It's our seventh volume—lucky number seven!

Thank you for supporting us all the way to this auspicious milestone!

The other day, I went strawberry picking for the first time in my life. I became a strawberry hunter, ravenously gobbling down delicious strawberries. As I prepared strawberries with condensed milk for my daughter to enjoy, I flashed back to a memory of my own childhood, when I was given the same treat. Suddenly I was overcome by wistful nostalgia.

And now I get to tie that anecdote into my volume 7 message!

Whether or not you've ever become a strawberry hunter, why not pick up this love comic and luxuriate in a strawberries-and-condensed-milk feeling?

Taishi Tsutsui

We Never Learn

We Never Learn

Volume 7 • SHONEN JUMP Manga Edition

STORY AND ART **Taishi Tsutsui**

TRANSLATION Camellia Nieh
SHONEN JUMP SERIES LETTERING Snir Aharon
GRAPHIC NOVEL TOUCH-UP ART & LETTERING Erika Terriquez
DESIGN Shawn Carrico
SHONEN JUMP SERIES EDITOR John Bae
GRAPHIC NOVEL EDITOR David Brothers

Printed in the U.S.A.

Published by VIZ Media, LLC
P.O. Box 77010
San Francisco, CA 94107

10 9 8 7 6 5 4 3 2 1
First printing, December 2019

VIZ MEDIA
viz.com

SHONEN JUMP
shonenjump.com

PARENTAL ADVISORY
WE NEVER LEARN is rated T+ for Older Teen and is recommended for ages 16 and up. This volume contains mild language and sexual themes.

RATED T+ OLDER TEEN
ratings.viz.com

[x] We + Never ÷ × Learn
7
They Express Words of [X] as a Diversion
Taishi Tsutsui
Where's Galiole!?

We Never Learn

Characters & Story

Nariyuki Yuiga and his family have led a humble life since his father passed away, with Yuiga doing everything he can to support his siblings. So when the principal of his school agrees to grant Nariyuki the school's special VIP recommendation for a full scholarship to college, he leaps at the opportunity. However, the principal's offer comes with one condition: Yuiga must serve as the tutor of Rizu Ogata, Fumino Furuhashi and Uruka Takemoto, the three girl geniuses who are the pride of Ichinose Academy! Unfortunately, the girls, while extremely talented in certain ways, all have subjects where their grades are absolutely rock-bottom. How will these three struggling students ever manage to pass their college entrance exams?!

Over the course of summer vacation, Nariyuki and all of the gang grow closer. By the time the second semester starts, they're on a first-name basis!

NARIYUKI YUIGA

A bright student from an ordinary family. Nariyuki lacks genius in any one subject but manages to maintain stellar grades through hard work. Agrees to take on the role of tutor in return for the school's special VIP recommendation.

CLASS:3-B

☺ Liberal Arts
☺ STEM
☹ Athletics

The Yuiga Family

A family of five consisting of Nariyuki, his mother and his siblings, Mizuki, Hazuki and Kazuki.

Kobayashi and Omori

Nariyuki's friends.

Inomori, Kashima and Chono

Members of the Thorn Club, Fumino's fan club!

Kawase and Umihara

Uruka's friends.

Ogata (Father)

Runs an udon shop. Dotes on his daughter.

RIZU OGATA

Known as the Thumbelina Supercomputer, Rizu is a math and science genius, but she's a dunce at literature, especially when human emotions come into play. She chooses a literary path to learn about human psychology—partially because she wants to become better at board games.

CLASS:3-F

☹ Liberal Arts ☺ STEM ☹ Athletics

FUMINO FURUHASHI

Known as the Sleeping Beauty of the Literary Forest, Fumino is a literary wiz whose mind goes completely blank when she sees numbers. She chooses a STEM path because she wants to study the stars.

CLASS:3-A

☺ Liberal Arts ☹ STEM ☺ Athletics

URUKA TAKEMOTO

Known as the Shimmering Ebony Mermaid Princess, Uruka is a swimming prodigy but is terrible at academics. In order to get an athletic scholarship, she needs to meet certain academic standards. She's had a crush on Nariyuki since junior high.

CLASS:3-D

☹ Liberal Arts ☹ STEM ☺ Athletics

MAFUYU KIRISU

A teacher at Ichinose Academy, and Rizu and Fumino's previous tutor. She believes people should choose their path according to their talents.

TEACHER

☺ Pedagogy

☹ Home Economics

ASUMI KOMINAMI

A graduate of Ichinose Academy. Works at a maid cafe and attends cram school in order to get into medical school and take over her father's clinic one day.

OG

☹ Science

☺ Service

TITLE

We Never Learn

CONTENTS

VOLUME 7 They Express Words of [*X*] as a Diversion

NAME Taishi Tsutsui

Question 52: Sometimes a Genius Pursues the Investigation of an Ignorant [X]

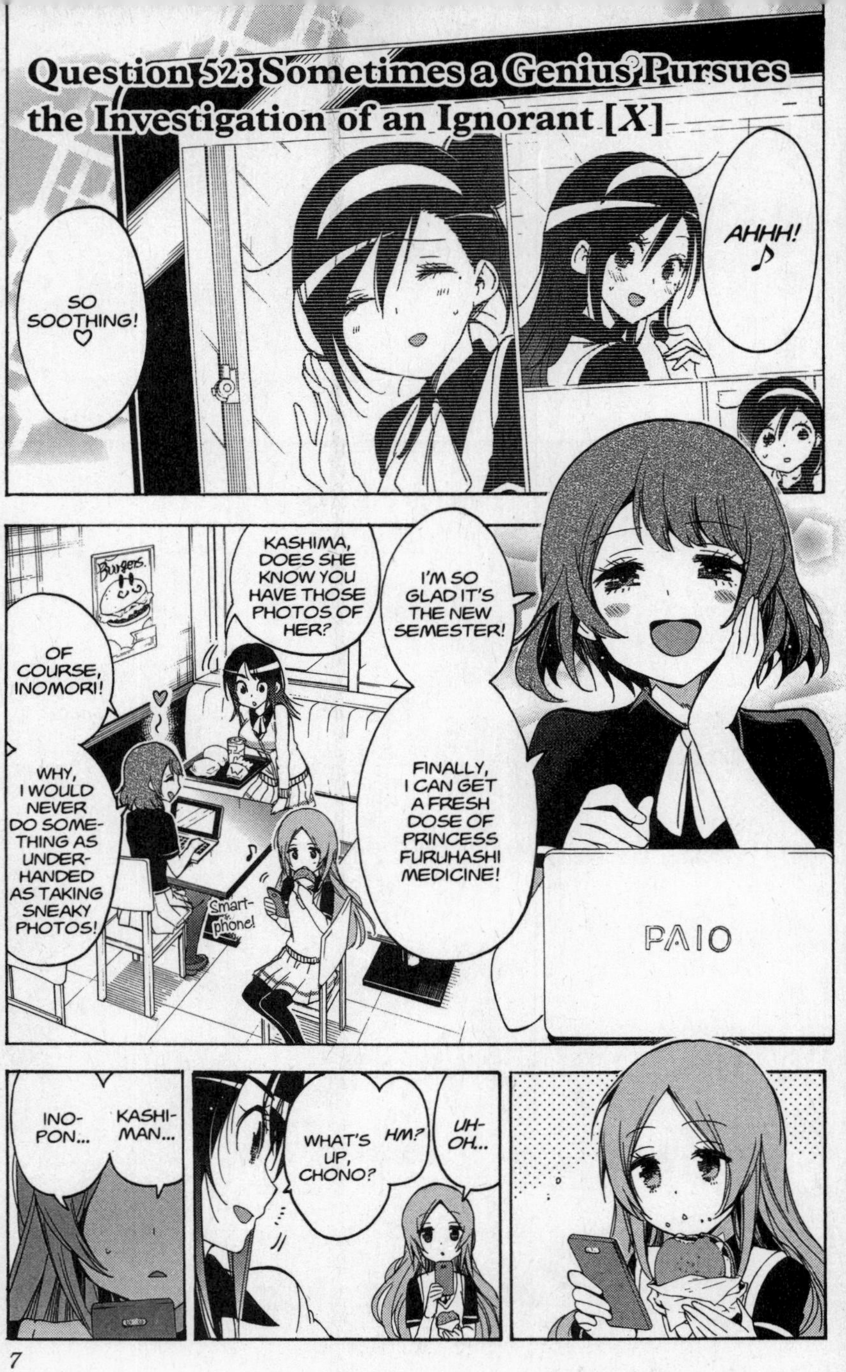

AHHH! ♪
SO SOOTHING! ♡
I'M SO GLAD IT'S THE NEW SEMESTER!
FINALLY, I CAN GET A FRESH DOSE OF PRINCESS FURUHASHI MEDICINE!
PAIO
KASHIMA, DOES SHE KNOW YOU HAVE THOSE PHOTOS OF HER?
OF COURSE, INOMORI!
WHY, I WOULD NEVER DO SOME-THING AS UNDER-HANDED AS TAKING SNEAKY PHOTOS!
Smart-phone!
Burgers
UH-OH...
HM?
WHAT'S UP, CHONO?
KASHI-MAN...
INO-PON...

THIS IS AN EMERGENCY!
DING DONG
DING DONG
CHIRP
CHIRP
3-A
GOOD MORN-ING!
YOU LOOK SLEEPY, FURU-HASHI!
GOOD MORNING...
Yawn...
IT WAS HARD TO WAKE UP—MY BRAIN'S STILL IN SUMMER-VACATION MODE!
AH HA HA!

FURU-HASHI...
OH!
GOOD MORNING, KASHIMA AND FRIENDS!
WHAT'S WRONG? YOU SEEM ANXIOUS...
FIDGET FIDGET
OH... WELL...
FIDGET
UM... HOW WAS...
...YOUR...
BLUSH
FIDGET
...SUMMER VACATION?
HUH? YOU'RE ASKING NOW?
WE'VE BEEN BACK AT SCHOOL THREE DAYS NOW!
WELL...
I WAS ONLINE YESTER-DAY...
...AND I HAP-PENED ACROSS...
...A CERTAIN INSTAGRAM ACCOUNT...
OH? WHADJA FIND?

4G
8:25
写真
spielen-with-love♡
ASUMA INN
ASUMA INN
spielen-with-love♡
I knew there was something going on between those two...♡

WHAAAAAAT?!
YAP YAP
THAT TIME AFTER THE FESTIVAL...?!
UM, FURUHASHI...
EASY NOW... CALM DOWN...
PSST
PSST
PSST
YOU'VE GOT IT ALL WRONG!
I CAN TOTALLY EXPLAIN!
OF COURSE! WE BELIEVE YOU!
Look me in the eye when you say that!
I DID SOME INVESTIGATING...
...BUT ALL I FOUND OUT WAS THAT THE ACCOUNT BELONGS TO A STUDENT AT OUR SCHOOL.
OH...
Geez, now what?
LUCKILY, THEY HAVE ZERO FOLLOWERS...
AT THIS POINT, I DOUBT ANYONE'S SEEN IT. BUT IT'S ONLY A MATTER OF TIME...
ONE OPTION IS TO RECRUIT A MASSIVE TEAM...
...AND TRACK THEM DOWN USING MASS-MOBILIZATION TACTICS.
PLEASE DON'T.
I'd rather do it myself.

BAM
BABABAM
WE'VE JUST GOT TO TRACK DOWN WHOEVER POSTED THIS...
...AND GET THEM TO DELETE IT, YUIGA!
SHOOP
Y-YEAH...
UM, YOU'RE REALLY CLOSE RIGHT NOW, FURUHASHI...
IF RICCHAN AND URUKA SEE THAT PHOTO...
OF COURSE, THERE WERE EXTENUATING CIRCUMSTANCES.
WORST CASE, IF PEOPLE FIND OUT, IF WE JUST EXPLAIN, IT SHOULD BE FINE.
Oog. My stomach...
CRMBL CRMBL
It will not be fine!!
This is a crisis, Yuiga!
I-I'M SORRY...
UM, YOU'RE STILL REALLY CLOSE, FURUHASHI!!

UM...
APART FROM THAT POST...
THEIR OTHER POSTS ARE MOSTLY OF CATS OR THE SKY OR DESSERTS ...
spielen-with-love
spielen-with-love♡
You know, no matter how badly people get hurt...a plate of dessert can bring back the milk of human kindness. Humans are nice like that...
BASED ON THE CAPTIONS ...
...THIS WAS PROBABLY WRITTEN BY A GIRL.
IF THIS IS ALL WE HAVE TO GO ON...
...I DON'T SEE HOW WE CAN TRACK HER DOWN...
...!
spielen-with-love
HEY, HOW DO YOU PRONOUNCE THIS ACCOUNT NAME?
SPI-E-LEN?
I get the "with love" part.
SPIELEN... THAT'S GERMAN.
I THINK IT MEANS...

TO PLAY MUSIC...
GASP
HUH?
MUSIC ROOM
THE DAY AFTER THE FESTIVAL?
EVERY-ONE IN THE BRASS BAND WAS AWAY AT A BAND EVENT DURING THAT TIME...
NOBODY WAS AROUND HERE.
Third-year students...
YEAH, EVERYONE TOOK PART.
I SEE ...
THANK YOU...
Sure.

WE TRIED THE ROCK MUSIC CLUB, THE CHOIR AND THE JAZZ CLUB TOO...
WORMP
THAT RULES OUT EVERYONE IN MUSIC ACTIVITIES AT OUR SCHOOL...
It seemed like a good lead, but...
WELL, THERE YOU HAVE IT.
I GUESS THERE ARE NO EASY ANSWERS ...
OKAY. LET'S GET BACK TO STUDY-ING!
NA-RI-YU-KI!
I know we need to study, but...
Yes...
CLATTER
GOOD WORK, EVERY-BODY!
LET'S TAKE A LITTLE BREAK!
I BROUGHT SOME TREATS!
Sweets & Cafe
Dolce & Haagen
YAAAY! THANK YOU!!
IT'S YOUR REWARD FOR HOW HARD YOU WORKED ON OUR LAST EXCURSION!
SQUEAL
WE LOVE YOU, SENSEI!
TAK TAK TAK TAK TAK
WE DON'T WANT TO INTERRUPT. LET'S GO.
YES...
Yay! Cake!
I want a Mont Blanc!

SHOOOP
HUH ?!
ZING
UM ...
WHAT'S UP...?
YANK
SNAP OUT OF IT, FURU-HASHI!!
I KNOW IT'S TEMPTING, BUT THOSE TREATS AREN'T FOR US!
HUH? NO, THAT'S NOT IT!
ALL OF THOSE DESSERTS ...
DROOL
...ARE THE SAME AS THE ONES IN THE INSTAGRAM ACCOUNT!
spielen-with-love♡
30 POSTS
0 FOLLOWERS
0 FOLLOWING
+ FOLLOW

IN OTHER WORDS, WE'VE IDENTIFIED THE CAKE SHOP THE POSTER FRE-QUENTS?!
I can't believe you spotted those cakes...
YES!!
WE'RE ZEROING IN ON THEM NOW!
WHAT ?!
...
WAIT ...
THESE PHOTOS OF DESSERTS ...
20xx July 30
...HAVE SOME-THING IN COM-MON.
20xx May 6
think I'll have cake again on my w
ome today!
20xx August 13
What a lovely taste!
Heading home with a full bell
20xx August 20
Cake should be eaten fresh ma
bakery!
It's the only way!
YEP, THIS ONE TOO... AND THIS ONE...
THEY'RE POSTED ON THE SAME DAY OF THE WEEK ...
THEY'RE ALL ON FRIDAYS! AND IT LOOKS LIKE SHE EATS AT THE SHOP...
ALSO ...
THERE'S A CRACK IN THE TABLE! IN EVERY PHOTO!!

DA DA DA DA DA
SO THAT MEANS...
EVERY FRIDAY, THIS PERSON...
...GOES TO THE SAME SHOP...
...AND HAS CAKE IN THE SAME SEAT!!
YAA-AAY!! RIGHT ON!
WELL DONE, NARI-YUKI!!
CHEW CHEW
CHEW CHEW CHEW
CHEW CHEW
CHEW CHEW
GEEZ, IS IT JUST THE CAKE...
...OR IS SOMETHING ELSE EXTRA SWEET?
BLUSH
HOW COME WE HAVE TO WATCH PEOPLE WHO AREN'T EVEN IN OUR CLUB FLIRTING?
I want a boyfriend.
AH, YOUNG LOVE!
WAY TO GO, EDUCATIONAL TUTOR!
SMAK
YEAH!!
Sweets & Cafe
Dolce & Haagen
Open
FRIDAY...
AFTER SCHOOL...

THIS IS DEFINITELY THE SPOT.
IF WE'VE READ THIS RIGHT...
...THE INSTAGRAM POSTER SHOULD SIT RIGHT OVER THERE!
TIK
TIK
TOK
TIK
TOK
STILL NO SIGN OF HER ...
WELL ...
... THERE'S NO GUARAN-TEE THAT SHE'LL SHOW...
COME TO THINK OF IT...

THIS IS THE FIRST TIME SINCE THAT DAY...
...THAT WE'VE BEEN ALONE TOGETHER.
NARI-YUKI...
I WONDER WHY...
...HE HELD MY HAND...
BUT YOU KNOW, FURU-HASHI...
IT'S LIKE PLAYING DETECTIVE. I'M HAVING FUN!
THIS KINDA SEEMS LIKE...
...WE'RE ON A DATE OR SOME-THING!

HUH?
NO!! WHY DID I SAY THAT?!
I MEAN ...
...THAT WAS ANOTHER ROLE-PLAYING EXERCISE IN FEMININE PSYCHOLOGY, YUIGA!
SHP
OH, UH... RIGHT!
It's been a while!
THANK YOU, PROFESSOR!
WHY, IF IT ISN'T YUIGA!
WHAT A COINCIDENCE!
WHOA !!
O-OMORI ?!
WHOA !!
YOU TOO, FURUHASHI ?!
HEY, DO YOU MIND IF I JOIN YOU?
UM, SURE, I GUESS ...
HA HA HA...GO RIGHT AHEAD!

YAY! LET'S SEE, WHAT'LL I HAVE? ♪
YOU'RE FUNNY, OMORI!
HEH HEH... NEVER MIND HIM.
LET'S FOCUS ON OUR GOAL.
Excuse me!
One order of the chocolate cake, please!
STILL NO SIGN OF THE POSTER...
YEAH...
Menu
Whee! ♡
KCHAK
MAYBE SHE'S NOT COMING TODAY...
HEY... I CAN STAY HERE AND WAIT LONGER.
YOU CAN GO, YUIGA...
TAPPA
TAPPA
DON'T BE SILLY!
WE'VE COME THIS FAR. WE'RE IN THIS TOGETHER!
YUIGA...
PING

spielen-with-love
Went with the chocolate this week! ♡ Ran into some friends and sat together—it's fun to mix it up at a different table sometimes! ♪
spielen-with-love♡
HUH? WHAT'S UP?
WHY ARE YOU BOTH STARING AT ME LIKE THAT?
SORRY, I'M NOT SHARING!
THIS IS MY SPECIAL ONCE-A-WEEK TREAT! ♡
THIS IS YOUR INSTAGRAM, OMORI!!
TALK ABOUT INCONGRUOUS!!
BA BA BAM
OMG, MY INSTAGRAM! DON'T LOOK! THAT'S EMBARRASSING!
IT'S A LITTLE LATE FOR THAT!
MORE IMPORTANTLY... THIS PHOTO!
SHOOP
YOU HAVE TO DELETE IT IMMEDIATELY!
ASUMA INN
ASUMA INN

AAAAAAH!
ZOOSH
RIIII-IIIGHT!!
?!
THAT MORNING...
I STAYED AT THAT INN WITH MY PARENTS...
...AND I HAPPENED TO WITNESS A SHOCKING SIGHT!
ASUMA INN
ASUMA INN
DEVASTATED WITH ENVY...
...I UPLOADED THE IMAGE TO INSTAGRAM...
LATER...
...PERHAPS AS A DEFENSE MECHANISM TO PROTECT MY EGO...
...I COMPLETELY OBLITERATED ALL MEMORY OF THE INCIDENT...
Say what?
GEEZ, YUIGA, YOU LUCKY DAWG!!
HOW COME SOME GUYS GET ALL THE BREAKS?!
And here you are together again. Gah!
IT'S NOT WHAT IT LOOKS LIKE...
PAT

*KANADERU MEANS "TO PLAY MUSIC" IN JAPANESE!

NOW ...
GRRR
HOW SHALL WE PUNISH HIM?
YIKES !!
KRAK
NEVER TAKE SNEAKY PHOTOS.

Question 53: Sometimes the Proximal [X] Is Green and Quick
Saegusa Seminar
All Japan Academics
Practice Test Hall
HEY, NARI-CHAN!
WELL, THAT'S FINISHED!
HEY, KOBAYASHI! HOW WAS IT FOR YOU?
Tch...
DON'T ASK!
NARI-CHAN, YOU'RE TAKING THE BUS BACK, RIGHT?
ARE YOU HEADING STRAIGHT HOME?
NO...
URUKA TOOK THE PRACTICE TEST TODAY TOO...
...SO I'LL HELP HER GO OVER HER ANSWERS FIRST...

WAIT, NARI-CHAN! SINCE WHEN ARE YOU TWO ON A FIRST-NAME BASIS?!
Dude, back off!
HEYA, NARIYUKI AND KOBAYAN!!
SORRY WE'RE LATE!
HEY, HAVEN'T SEEN YOU SINCE THE MEET, YUIGA!
HEY, IT'S BEEN A WHILE!
HI, UMIHARA! YOU HERE FOR THE PRACTICE TEST TOO?
Long time no see!
Ha ha ha!
WOW, IT'S LIKE A JUNIOR HIGH REUNION!
HOW WAS THE PRACTICE TEST?
SHUMP
WORMP
OH, THAT BAD?
WELL, LET'S REVIEW.

GEE...
I WORKED THIS PRACTICE WORKBOOK ALL SUMMER.
I FELT PRETTY CONFIDENT...
ALL JAPAN ACADEMICS
PRACTICE TEST
SAMPLE QUESTIONS BY LEVEL
ENGLISH
SHOULD I GET A NEW ONE?
...
NO...
I DON'T THINK YOU NEED A NEW WORKBOOK NOW.
You'll just get more confused.
I THINK RIGHT NOW WE NEED TO DIG DEEPER.
Practice Test
FOR EXAMPLE, TAKE THESE MULTIPLE-CHOICE QUESTIONS.
YOU KNOW HOW TO SOLVE THEM IN THIS FORMAT...
...BUT NOT WHEN THEY'RE PUT INTO DIFFERENT QUESTIONS.
A) discourage
B) rescue
A) astonished
B) scared
C) impressed
D) bored
HUH?
SO...

FROM NOW ON...
I WANT YOU TO ACTUALLY WRITE THE WORDS IN ENGLISH IN THE BLANKS.
RIGHT!
CHECK THE JAPANESE TRANSLATIONS OF THE QUESTIONS TO SEE IF YOU REALLY UNDERSTAND THE GRAMMAR.
THAT'S HOW WE DIG DEEPER.
YES, YES.
HONESTLY, THIS AP-PROACH...
...IS TOTALLY RIPPED OFF FROM ASHU... I MEAN, KOMINAMI SENPAI.
REALLY?
HEH
HEH
LATER, NARI-CHAN!
SEE YOU AT SCHOOL!
deadline: end of December
OH? DON'T YOU WANT TO STAY AND REVIEW WITH US?
YOU'RE SUCH A NERD, NARI-CHAN!
Practice Test English
HEY, URUKA!
THIS IS YOUR CHANCE... YOU'LL BE ALONE TOGETHER!
PUSH PUSH
AT LEAST KISS HIM. MINIMUM!

UUUUU-MICCHI!!
I CAN'T DO THAT! GAH!!
HA HA HA! YOU'VE GOT THIS, CAPTAIN TAKEMOTO!
Fare thee well!
BADMP
BADMP
BADMP
YEESH...
THAT UMICCHI... AND HER IDEAS...
YOU TWO SEEM CLOSE.
deadline: end of December
10th
YEAH... I GUESS SO.
UMICCHI AND KAWACCHI HAVE BEEN MY PALS SINCE JUNIOR HIGH...
SPEAKING OF WHICH...
YOU AND KOBAYAN HAVE BEEN BUDDIES SINCE GRADE SCHOOL, NO?
Right?
YEAH.
BOTH OF HIS PARENTS WORK TOO...
...SO HE USED TO COME OVER A LOT AND HELP LOOK AFTER MY LITTLE SISTER.
National
English
WOW...

LEVEL
Practice Test
SO KOBAYAN ...
...MUST KNOW A LOT ABOUT NARI-YUKI...
...THAT I'VE NEVER EXPERI-ENCED.
YOU'VE JUST GOTTA ATTACK!
GUH
I WISH I KNEW NARIYUKI BETTER...
OKAY.. MAYBE TODAY...
I'LL TRY TO BE A BIT PROAC-TIVE...
URUKA...
ABOUT THIS QUESTION YOU MISSED...
National Mitaka Seminar Practice Test English
YAYYY
OR MAYBE NOT TODAY!!
I'M ALREADY SO HAPPY!
TODAY IS GOOD!!
HEH
UM, ARE YOU LISTEN-ING?
HEY... URUKA?

GEE...
WE MADE A LOT OF PROGRESS TODAY.
YEAH! ♪
THANK YOU, NARIYUKI!
THAT'S RIGHT.
EVEN JUST THE FACT THAT HE CALLS ME BY MY FIRST NAME...
...IS A HUGE STEP FORWARD!
I ROCK!
HUH?
?
OVER THERE ON THAT BENCH... ISN'T THAT KOBAYASHI AND UMIHARA?
OH! YOU'RE RIGHT!
I THOUGHT THEY WENT HOME!
HEY—

BADUMP BADUMP BADUMP
BADUMP BADUMP BADUMP
HEY ...
ARE THOSE TWO...
Y-YEAH...
IT'S PRETTY OBVIOUS ...
BADUMP BADUMP BADUMP BADUMP
OH! HARUMA!
IT'S ALMOST TIME FOR THE BUS!
HOPPITY
YES, WE'D BETTER GO, CHINAMI!
TMP TMP TMP TMP

WHAAAAAT?!
OMG!
I THOUGHT I WAS GONNA SUFFOCATE!!
I...
I HAD NO IDEA!
KOBAYASHI... HAS A GIRLFRIEND?
FOR REAL?
BA-DMP BA-DMP
I HAD NO CLUE EITHER!
UMICCHI DIDN'T SAY ANYTHING...
BA-DMP BA-DMP
OOH...
I CAN'T BELIEVE WE SAW THAT...
GASP GASP
...
...
ANYWAY...
...THE BUS...
SHOULD WE WAIT FOR THE NEXT ONE?
NO OBJECTIONS HERE...

BRRRMM
THIS IS...
...SO AWKWARD!
SHEESH...
FEELS LIKE MY OLD FRIEND SUDDENLY GREW UP.
WELL, IT MAKES SENSE.
KOBA-YASHI'S A GOOD GUY, AND HE'S HAND-SOME, TOO.
...ISS...
HUH?

OH YEAH...
NARI-YUKI...
YOU'VE ALREADY ...
... KISSED SOME-ONE TOO...
N-NO.
THAT WASN'T REALLY A KISS.
IT DOESN'T COUNT.
IT WAS MORE OF AN ACCI-DENT.
YEAH.
I GET IT.

NEXT STOP, FUTA-TSUBA HIGH SCHOOL.
ER...
PRESS THE BUZZER TO STOP AT FUTA-TSUBA HIGH SCHOOL.
...
I GUESS ...
NOD
NOD
...MY TIME WILL COME TOO.
NOW PASSING FUTA-TSUBA HIGH SCHOOL.
I GUESS ...
SNOOZE
...I'LL EXPERIENCE SOMETHING SIMILAR ONE DAY...
NARI-YUKI...
...ARE YOU ASLEEP?
MM...

HUH?
BADMP
NARI ... ... YUKI...
HUH?
BA-DMP
BA-DMP
WHA...
BA-DMP
WHAT ?!

BA-DMP
URU...
BUMPA
BRRMM
...
...?!
DROOL
WHA ...
WHAT'S UP, NARI-YUKI?
DID SOME-THING STARTLE YOU?

THE NEXT STOP IS NANAO DISTRICT CENTER.
PLEASE PRESS THE BUZZER TO STOP AT NANAO DISTRICT CENTER..
DING DONG
OH!
OUR STOP IS NEXT, NARI-YUKI!
...
WAS IT A DREAM?!
WHAT?!
WHERE'D THAT COME FROM?!
I'M SO EMBAR-RASSED!!
WHAT'S WRONG?
DID YOU HAVE A WEIRD DREAM?
YEAH, KIND OF.
OH...
WHAT DID YOU DREAM?
BADMP

I...
NOTHING, OKAY! NOTHING!!
BLUSH
GEE, YOU'RE ACTING WEIRD, NARI-YUKI.
OOG...
WOW, THAT WAS SO IN-TENSE!
...
BA DMP
BA DMP
BA DMP
THE NEXT DAY...
HA HA HA HA!
I WAS BUMMED OUT AFTER THE SWIM MEET THIS SUMMER...
AND HARUMA— I MEAN, KOBAYASHI— WAS TRYING TO CHEER ME UP...
...AND ONE THING LED TO ANOTHER...

SORRY I DIDN'T TELL YOU SOONER!
I MEANT TO TELL YOU, BUT IT FELT AWKWARD!
ROMANCE IS IN THE AIR!
Ha ha!
CONGRATULATIONS, UMICCHI!
SO?
HAVE YOU ALREADY KISSED?
...
3-B
WH ...
WHAT?! KOBAYASHI !!
WITH UMIHARA, IN CLASS D?
YOU LUCKY JERK!!
CONGRATULATIONS, KOBAYASHI.
Calm down, dude.
DIDJA ALREADY KISS, KOBAYASHI, YOU DAWG?!
DIDJA DO IT? DIDJA?
WELL ...
THAT'S A SECRET. ♡
WHAAAT?!
...
BADMP BADMP BADMP
DRIP DRIP DRIP

THIRTY YEARS AS A BUS DRIVER
HEISA-BURO OSHIMA
BRRRMM
THE ONLY MAN WHO KNOWS THE TRUTH...

Question 54: At Times, an Elder's Pride Is in Direct Opposition to [X]'s Circumstances

*IN JAPAN, GIRLS GIVE SWEETS TO BOYS ON VALENTINE'S DAY, AND BOYS REPAY THE FAVOR ON WHITE DAY!

BRRRMM
HEY, KOHAI ...
YOU'D BETTER REALLY HOLD ON. IT'S DANGER-OUS OTHER-WISE.
OH, RIGHT. SORRY.
GEE... SO SOFT...
SKWEEZ
BRRMMM
SEVERAL HOURS...
... EARLIER ...

High Stage
ハイステージ
A MAID HOUSE-KEEPING SERVICE?
WHAT'RE YOU TALKING ABOUT?
IT'S JUST WHAT IT SOUNDS LIKE. A MAID COMES TO YOUR HOUSE AND CLEANS IT.
IT'S A NEW SERVICE WE'RE OFFERING.
For real?
WE'RE GETTING WAY MORE ORDERS THAN WE EXPECTED.
WE'RE SHORT-HANDED!
YOU'RE GOOD AT HOUSE-KEEPING, RIGHT, YUIGA?
IF YOU COULD SUPPORT ASHUMI, THAT WOULD BE A BIG HELP!
YOU'LL BE PAID, OF COURSE!
Doesn't hurt to ask!
I TOLD YOU, I DON'T NEED ANY HELP!
I DON'T MIND. YOU'VE HELPED ME PLENTY!
EEK! ♡ YOU'RE SO DREAMY, YUIGA! ♡
DID EITHER OF YOU EVEN LISTEN?!
YIKES!

END OF FLASHBACK...
SORRY TO TROUBLE YOU WITH THIS, RUNT.
BANK
I DON'T KNOW WHY THEY INSISTED...
BRRRRMM
NO PROBLEM. BUT I AM A BIT NERVOUS.
WELL ...
ALL YOU HAVE TO DO IS ASSIST ME.
I'LL TAKE FULL RESPONSIBILITY.
YOU'RE SO COOL, ASHUMI SENPAI!
I TOLD YOU NOT TO CALL ME THAT!
CHECK THE ADDRESS ON THE ORDER, WOULDJA?
SURE ...
THE FIRST ADDRESS ON THE LIST IS...
RUSTLE
...
HUH?

HUH?
MAFUYU SENSEI?
OH, NOW I SEE!
IT SAYS "KIRISU" ON THE ORDER SHEET.
KOMI-NAMI...
WHAT ARE YOU DOING HERE?
I'M YOUR HOUSE-KEEPING SERVICE. DUH!
NOW, MAY WE COME IN?
TUG
TUGGA TUGGA TUGGA TUGGA

UM, SENSEI?
IF YOU DON'T LET GO OF THE DOOR, WE CAN'T DO OUR JOB.
KOMI-NAMI...
SHOOP
...
WHAT'S THIS?
PAYMENT.
A REWARD.
ALL I ASK IS THAT YOU GO HOME AND NOT SPEAK OF THIS AGAIN.
WHAT ...
WHAT DO YOU TAKE ME FOR?!
I TAKE PRIDE IN MY WORK! I COULD NEVER ACCEPT PAYMENT WITHOUT DOING MY JOB!!
WHAT SHOULD I DO...?
Let me in!
TUGGA TUGGA TUGGA
Go home!
RRMBBBB
GASP

SHP
HUH?
HUH?
JUST ...
...30 MINUTES ...
TUG
JUST GIVE ME 30 MINUTES, PLEASE !!
KASLAM
KIDDOOOO!
Whoa!! How'd it get so bad in such a short time?!
Huh?! Your dignity...as a teacher...?
Sigh...
Whoa! Eel and rice bowl ?!
KLATTER
SKWEEK SKWEEK
KLUNKA KLUNKA
VRRRRRR

THIRTY MINUTES LATER...
KCHAK
WHSH
SORRY TO KEEP YOU WAITING.
YOU MAY CLEAN NOW.
GLEAM
...
SWF
Hff
Hff
SPARKLE SPARKLE SPARKLE

THERE'S NOTHING LEFT TO DO!!
IS THIS SUP-POSED TO BE SOME KIND OF JOKE, SENSEI?!
APOLO-GIES!
I'M JUST A SLAVE TO MY FASTIDIOUS NATURE!
NEXT!!
LET'S MOVE ON TO THE NEXT PLACE, SENPAI!
Am I really hearing this?!
TAKEMOTO
HOW DO YOU FEEL, MOM?
I'LL TAKE CARE OF ALL THE COOKING AND CLEANING TODAY.
YOU JUST REST!
KOFF KOFF
URUKA...
BUT YOU'RE EXHAUSTED, BETWEEN SWIM PRACTICE AND YOUR STUDIES...
I DON'T WANT YOU TO WORRY ABOUT HOUSE-WORK...
Wheez wheez
...SO I CALLED A HOUSE-KEEPING SERVICE!
SWIM

I DIDN'T KNOW THERE WAS SUCH A THING.
BUT I AM PRETTY BEAT. I GUESS THIS IS BETTER...
Wobble wobble
KNOCK
KNOCK
DING DOONG
KCHACK
HELLO?
NARIYUKI AND KOMINAMI SENPAI?!
W-WHY ARE YOU DRESSED LIKE THAT?!
Heya, Uruka...
WHAT?!
WE'RE AT TAKE-MOTO'S HOUSE NOW?!
LET'S SEE... THE ORDER SAYS...
CLEANING THE HOUSE AND PREPARING DINNER.
LET'S PROCEED...
RIGHT! WE'VE GOT THIS!
EXCUSE US!
UMM UHH

EEEEEEK!!
WHAT'S GOING ON?! AS IF KOMINAMI SENPAI WASN'T ENOUGH...
EXCUSE US...
Let's do this!
NARI-YUKI IS IN MY HOUSE?!
HUH?!
SHP
SHP
WAAAAH!!
WHAT'LL I DO?! WHAT'LL I DO?!
SWOOSH
CHOP
WHAT'LL I DO?!
WHAT'LL I DO?!
CHOP CHOP
CHOP CHOP
OTOME
WHAT'LL I DO?!
WHAT'LL I DO?!
OTOME

MMM...
YES ...
DELI-CIOUS!
IT'S EXTREMELY DIFFICULT TO MAKE A BROTH THIS DELICATE...
TEE HEE... YOU REALLY THINK SO?
GEE, THANKS!
WAIT... WHY ARE WE GETTING SERVED?!
AAA-AAH!! I'M SORRY!!
I GOT CARRIED AWAY AND JUST DID EVERY-THING!
GAAAAAH!!
WHERE'S MY WORK?!
NEXT!!
WE'LL GET THE NEXT ONE, SENPAI!!

Furuhashi
WHAT'S UP WITH THIS LIST?!
NOTHING WILL SURPRISE ME NOW...
UM...
I DID ORDER A HOUSE-KEEPING SERVICE ...
BUT... KOMINAMI SENPAI... IN A MAID OUTFIT?!
NEVER MIND THAT, FURU-HASHI.
HAVE YOU GOT SOME WORK FOR US?
Please, just let us work quick!
OH...
R-RIGHT!
WELL, ACTUALLY, THE KITCHEN IS A MESS.
I'M AT MY WIT'S END...
AND I'M STARV-ING...

OH!
FURUHASHI'S A WORLD-CLASS ACE AT ALL OF THE FEMININE ARTS...
WHY WOULD SHE CALL A HOUSE-KEEPING SERVICE?!
NARIYUKI'S SINCERELY PERPLEXED FACE!!
THIS IS... AWFUL!!
I MADE A LONG-OVERDUE ATTEMPT AT COOKING AGAIN, AND THE KITCHEN IS A TOTAL DISASTER!
AS A GIRL, HOW CAN I POSSIBLY LET A BOY SEE THIS?
IT'S THE ULTIMATE NO-NO!
FWIP
SPLUT

GROVEL
THAT WILL BE ALL. THANK YOU.
Please go.
THIS AGAIN ?!
WHAT'S THE DEAL?! YOU'RE HUNGRY, RIGHT?!
OOG!
I'M STUFFED!
GRRWWWLLL
LIAR !!
LISTEN, I TAKE PRIDE IN MY WORK AS A MAID!
...I REFUSE TO LEAVE A CLIENT HUNGRY!
KOMI-NAMI SEN-PAI...
GGRRWL
IF I'M GETTING PAID...
GRRWL
ER, YES ...
YOU GET IT, RIGHT?
LLWRG
BIP

AT YOUR SERVICE.
THREE ORDERS...
...OF UDON.
OGATA UDON
OGATA UDON
WHA ...
GRRWWLL
WHAT'S GOING ON?!
HMPH! THIS UDON IS DELI-CIOUS...
SLRP
SLRPA
THIS IS OUR SECOND DINNER...
THERE'S SECONDS, TOO.
I'M SORRY! I'M SORRY!
I had no choice!!

WORMP
WHAT A TOTAL BUST...
WE DIDN'T DO ANYTHING.
THERE, THERE...
THESE THINGS HAPPEN ...
I'M GOING THIS WAY NOW...
SHUP
HUH?
SPARKLE
SPARKLE
SPARKLE
OH...
WOW ...
SPARKLE
SPARKLE

WHOA !!
SHOOOF
THAT MAID-COSTUME LADY IS AWESOME!
WHEN'RE YOU GONNA MARRY HER?
YES, WHEN SHOULD WE TIE THE KNOT, DARLING?
CUT THAT OUT! THEY'LL TAKE YOU SERIOUSLY!
MELT...
ER, SENPAI? YOU DON'T HAVE TO DO ALL THIS...
I DON'T MIND.
I'M JUST NOT OKAY WITH GETTING PAID FOR NOTHING!
Well, thanks...
YOUR HOUSE'LL DO. JUST LET ME BE USEFUL!
ZZZ
HERE.
PAT

YOUR TURN.
PAT PAT
WHAAAAT?! I COULDN'T POSSIBLY...
BLUSH
ZING
HURRY UP!
I'VE HAD ENOUGH FRUSTRATION FOR ONE DAY!
DOES THAT FEEL GOOD, RUNT?
Y-YES...
LET ME KNOW IF THERE'S AN ITCHY SPOT.
OKAY...
NORMALLY THIS SERVICE COSTS A LOT TO ADD ON!
E-EXCUSE ME...
...

PSST...
BUT...
WELL ...
FOR YOU...
...I'LL DO IT FOR FREE ANY DAY.
CUT THAT OUT!
I'M NOT FALLING FOR THAT AGAIN!
AW, PHOOEY ...
I WAS HOPING FOR A CUTER REACTION, KOHAI.
Booooring!
THE NEXT DAY...
COME TO THINK OF IT...
I DIDN'T REALIZE KOMINAMI SENPAI WAS WORKING AS A MAID...
DID YOU KNOW, NARIYUKI?
WELL, UM...I...
STARE

WHA ?!
BIG BRO'S EARS ARE ALL CLEAN!
YOU NOTICED THAT FROM ACROSS THE ROOM?!

Question 55: They Express Words of [X] as a Diversion

HE'S BLUSHING!
YOU LOSE, YUIGA!
ZAP
Yeah!
WHAA-AT?!
WHAT KINDA GAME IS THIS?!
YOU MEAN YOU'RE IN HIGH SCHOOL AND YOU DON'T KNOW THE "I LOVE YOU" GAME?
YOU'LL NEVER BE POPULAR UNTIL YOU LEARN!
PERSON A SAYS, "I LOVE YOU." PERSON B SAYS, "AGAIN." WHOEVER GETS EMBARRASSED FIRST LOSES!
I love you!
Again!
WHAT A CRAZY GAME!
Sheesh...
WE'VE DECIDED ...
...TO CAPITALIZE ON THE TREND!
I LOVE YOU GAME
1 round 2,000 yen
PRIZE FOR BEATING A MAID:
飲食
3,000 YEN VOUCHER
FOR FOOD AND DRINK!
HIGH STAGE
SHF
A 3,000-YEN VOUCHER IF YOU BEAT A MAID?
ARE YOU SURE ABOUT THAT?
Business-wise...
ASHUMI, YOU HAVE I LOVE YOU GAME CUSTOMERS!

YAY!! I'LL DO MY VERRRRRRY BEST! ♡
PAH
I LOVE YOU! ♡
BLUSH
I WIN AGAIN!
IT WAS WORTH IT!
ASHUMI'S UNBEATABLE AT THIS GAME!
TEE-HEE! ♡
She's good...
HEH
CHA-CHING

SO IN THIS CASE, THE ANTICIPATED VALUE OF E (X)...
$E(X) = \sum_{k=1}^{N} x_k p_k = x_1 p_1 + x_2 p_2 + \ldots + x_N p_N$
MUNCH MUNCH
RIGHT!
SHFF
SKRIT
SKRIT
I LOVE YOU!
AGA—!
CRAP. I LOSE.
GAME OVER!
YOU'RE KIDDING ME...
SO... THIS GAME REALLY IS POPULAR?
?
THE I LOVE YOU GAME?
ARE YOU INTERESTED IN IT, NARIYUKI?
NO, THAT'S NOT IT...

RIGHT ON! LET'S TRY THIS!!
BAAAAM
HUH ?!
WHERE'D YOU COME FROM, OMORI?!
I'M A PRO AT THIS GAME, YOU DUMMY!
I'VE ALWAYS WANTED TO TRY IT WITH A GIRL!
Huh?
SO WHO DID YOU PLAY TO BECOME A PRO?
Heya, Omoricchi!
I DON'T REALLY GET IT, BUT...
...IF IT'S A GAME, I WANT TO TRY.
I'LL DO IT...
RRRMMMB
HMPH
YAY!
RMMMB
OGATA'S GAMER SPIRIT IS ON FIRE!

I LOVE YOU.
BRING IT ON!
DEADPAN
I LOVE YOU.
AGAIN! ♪
DEADPAN
I LOVE YOU.
AGAIN! ♡
DEADPAN
SPLOSH
OMG, I LOSE!!
BUT I'M SO GLAD TO BE ALIVE!
WHATTA PRO...
DEADPAN
I love you.
DEADPAN
I love you.
DEADPAN
I love you.
RIZURIN. YOU'RE LIKE A BROKEN RECORD.
GASP
THAT'S THE FIRST GAME I'VE EVER WON!!
I WANT TO PLAY YOU NEXT, NARIYUKI!
SHOOSH
WHAT?!
I CAN FINALLY GET YOU BACK FOR BEATING ME AT NIMUTO!
IT'S A SHOW-DOWN!
YOU'RE STILL HOLDING ON TO THAT?!

I'm just learning...
READY, SET...
GO!
HUFF HUFF
ALL I HAVE TO DO IS REPEAT A FEW WORDS.
THERE'S NO RATIONAL REASON I SHOULD LOSE.
SHOULD BE A BREEZE.
I...
I...
L...
HUH?
WHAT'S WRONG?
YOU CAN START, RIZURIN...
?
?

SHAKA SHAKA
I L-L-L-L-L-L-L-L-L-L...
OGATA BROKE DOWN!!
SHE'S A DIF-FERENT KIND OF BROKEN RECORD NOW!!
WOOHOO
YUIGA WINS!!
WHAT? I WON?
HE BEAT THE THUMBELINA CLOCKWORK MACHINE?!
PSHOO
HOW'D HE DO THAT?!
RICCHAN, YOU'RE SO CUTE...
TEE-HEE...
MMM?!
WELL THEN...
DAH
?!
OF COURSE...
IT'S YOUR TURN NEXT, FURU-HASHI!
HEH HEH

KASHIMA AND EVERYONE?
WHERE'D YOU COME FROM?!
IT'S LUNCH BREAK. WHY SHOULDN'T WE BE HERE?
NOW, LET'S DO THIS!
PSST PSST
THIS IS YOUR CHANCE TO GET CLOSER TO HIM!
KRIK
I'm not trying to get closer!
SHEESH!
WELL, LET'S GET THIS OVER WITH SO WE CAN STUDY!
ALL RIGHT. LET'S GO, YUIGA.
BRING IT ON, FURUHASHI!
I LOVE ...

STARE
GUH GUH GUH GUH
HOW CAN I SAY IT IN FRONT OF THESE TWO?!
UM... ER...
THIS IS EMBARRASSING ...
FURUHASHI ADMITS DEFEAT!
WHOOAAA!
THAT'S TWO IN A ROW!
AM I GOOD AT THIS ?!
YOU JERK, YOU'RE SO CLUELESS!
STOMACH MEDICINE

THIS TIME IT'S YOUR TURN TO SAY "I LOVE YOU."
HOW ABOUT MAKING A PENALTY DARE FOR THE LOSER THIS TIME?
SURE! LET'S DO IT!
HEY... NARIYUKI'S GETTING A LITTLE COCKY NOW!
OKAY ...
I WANNA PLAY!
I'LL GO NEXT!
ALL RIGHT! TAKE-MOTO STEPS UP TO THE PLATE!!
WELL, WELL!
YOU'RE MY NEXT CHAL-LENGER, URUKA?
Watch out!
HEH HEH!
GO EASY ON ME, NARIYUKI!
ARE YOU SURE ABOUT THIS, URUKA?
THERE'S A PENALTY IF YOU LOSE...
NO SWEAT!

SHING
AFTER ALL...
...THIS IS THE CHANCE OF A LIFE-TIME!
RRRUMBBB
IF I GET TO HEAR NARIYUKI SAY "I LOVE YOU" TO ME...
BEGIN!
BADMP BADMP
IT'S WORTH HAVING TO TAKE ON A PENALTY!!
*SHE'S NOT EVEN EX-PECT-ING TO WIN!
BRING IT ON!
GO FOR IT, NARIYUKI!
SHAH
UM...
PSHOOO
UM... ER...
...
FIDGET FIDGET
WHAT?
Okay. You lose.
COME ON AND SAY IT...

YEAH!
YUIGA LOSES! THE PENALTY DARE'S ON YOU!
YAHOO!
YOU HAVE TO PLAY THE I LOVE YOU GAME WITH THE NEXT PERSON WHO WALKS INTO THE CLASSROOM! ♪
GAHHH !!
WORMP
N-N-N-NO WAY! THAT'S INSANE !!
EEP
EEP
A MAN DOESN'T GO BACK ON HIS WORD, YUIGA!!
Wanna go study in another classroom?
Sure.
Want some udon?
HEY! SOME-ONE'S HERE!
TAK TAK
Woo-hoo ♪
UGH!
PLEASE... LET IT BE A DUDE!
OR IF NOT, AT THE VERY LEAST...
...LET IT BE SOMEONE WHO WILL LAUGH IT OFF!!
CLATTER

WHAT A RUCKUS ...
I KNOW IT'S LUNCH-TIME, BUT SHOULDN'T YOU SENIORS BE STUDY-ING?
GREAT... THE PERSON LEAST LIKELY TO LAUGH IT OFF!
THE ICE QUEEN, KIRISU SEN-SEI!
THAT'S ASKING TOO MUCH ...
YEAH, WE CAN'T HOLD HIM TO THIS...
PSST
...
UM, SENSEI ...
WOULD YOU MIND...
... SITTING DOWN HERE?
TREMBL
SHIVR
TREMBL
?
HE'S DOING IT!!
OMG, YUIGA, ARE YOU FOR REAL?!

WHAT IS IT?
TREMBL
TREMBL
TREMBL
ADVICE ON YOUR FUTURE PATH?
UM...
I...
ER...
I LOVE YOU.

A-
I'M SORRY .....
I ADMIT DEFEAT.
SHUDDR SHUDDR SHAKA SHAKA
AGAIN?
I COULDN'T HEAR YOU VERY WELL.
COME AGAIN?
ER... AM I SAFE?
YUIGA ...
TAK TAK TAK
TWITCH
AFTER SCHOOL ...
...COME SEE ME IN THE STUDENT INSTRUCTION ROOM.
GLARE
BUSTED!!

CLATTER CLATTER
PSHAA
...
...
YUIGA, YOU'RE THE MAN!
A MAN AMONG MEN!!
...
WORMP
SORRY FOR PUTTING YOU THROUGH THAT!
WE'LL BUY YOU A STEAMED BUN, OKAY?
STUDENT INSTRUCTION ROOM
I SEE ...
IT WAS PART OF A GAME...
I UNDER-STAND THAT PART.

BUT ... WHAT'S FUN ABOUT THAT?
I'M SORRY.
I DON'T REALLY GET IT EITHER.
SIGH...
RIDICU-LOUS.
I LO...
I'M SORRY.
IT MAY BE A GAME, BUT I FIND THE WHOLE THING...
... RIDICU-LOUS.
GAME OR NO GAME...
A STUDENT AND TEACHER...
...HAVE NO BUSINESS SAYING THOSE WORDS TO EACH OTHER.

YOU'RE RIGHT.
I GOT CARRIED AWAY.
IT WAS TOTALLY INAPPROPRIATE.
OBVIOUSLY.
I HOPE YOU'LL MAKE BETTER CHOICES IN THE FUTURE.
UM...
AND SINCE WE'RE TEACHER AND STUDENT...
...I GUESS I SHOULDN'T BE CLEANING UP YOUR APARTMENT ANYMORE.
...
SENSEI?
DID YOU HEAR ME, SENSEI?
...
WELL, YUIGA...
...THOSE ARE TWO SEPARATE THINGS!

IS THE I LOVE YOU GAME BIG AT YOUR SCHOOL TOO, MIZUKI?
WHAT? COULD YOU SAY THAT AGAIN?
THE I LOVE YOU GAME.
THE WHAT GAME?
THE I LOVE YOU GAME.

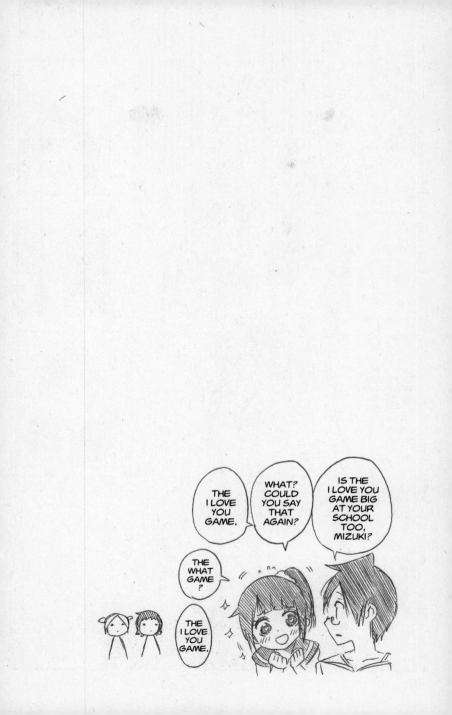

Question 56: Sometimes Fate Leads a Predecessor to Wrestle with [X]

MEMO-RIZATION...
THE KEY TO LEARNING NEW INFOR-MATION...
...IS TO ASSOCIATE IT WITH THINGS WE ALREADY KNOW.
ALL OF US...
...QUICKLY FORGET INFORMATION STORED IN SHORT-TERM MEMORY.
IN ORDER TO MAKE OUR LEARNING MEANINGFUL...
...WE CAN USE A TRICK TO RECORD IT DEEP IN OUR LONG-TERM MEMORY.
ASSOCIATING NEW INFORMATION WITH THINGS WE ALREADY KNOW...
...HELPS US TO ESTABLISH IT IN OUR LONG-TERM MEMORY.
Glance
...
SO, BEARING THAT IN MIND...
DROOP
DROOP

ZZZ
ZZZ
PSST! FURU-HASHI!
TAP TAP
MMF...
WHA-?!
I'M SOOO LOOKING FORWARD TO TOMOR-ROW'S MINI-TEST. AREN'T YOU, FURUHASHI?
RRMBBB
WAAAAH! I'M SO SORRY!!
DIIING DOOONG
OOF... I TOTALLY GOT BUSTED...
I KNEW IT... SENSEI HATES ME...
I know... it's my own fault.
WELL... YOU KNOW... IT'S THE SECOND SEMESTER NOW...
I'M SURE SHE'S JUST WORRIED ABOUT YOU.
Maybe...

TAP TAP
TAP TAP
TAP
TAP
TAP TAP TAP
HMPH ... MAKING THIS MINI-TEST...
...IS TAKING LONGER THAN I EXPECTED.
I'VE BEEN SHORT ON SLEEP LATELY...
I WAS HOPING TO GET TO BED EARLY TONIGHT...
TAP
ALMOST DONE...

SHP
ZZZT
It was un-plugged!
...
THE BAT-TERY'S DEAD...
NOW WHEN ...
...DID I LAST SAVE?
CHIRP
CHIRP
CHIRP
SKRIT
SKRIT

WORLD HISTORY
MINI-TEST
GRRR
GRR
GEE... KIRISU SENSEI ...
... SEEMS SCARIER THAN USUAL TODAY...
WORLD HISTORY
MINI-TEST
GRR
ALMOST LIKE SHE MIGHT CHOKE US IF WE FAIL TO FOCUS ON THE MINI-TEST...
SKRIT
GRR
FOCUS... FOCUS...
SKRIT
SKRIT
TIK
SAIKO
TIK
TIK
TIK
TIK
TIK
TIK

JERK
SHOOSH
UN...
UNACCEPTABLE!!
BADMP BADMP
I MAY HAVE PULLED AN ALL-NIGHTER, BUT A TEACHER HAS NO BUSINESS FALLING ASLEEP IN CLASS!!
SKWEEZ
SO IRONIC... AFTER I CAME DOWN ON FURUHASHI SO HARD YESTERDAY FOR THE SAME THING!
Focus...
SKRIT SKRIT SKRIT SKRIT
LUCKILY...
...NONE OF THE STUDENTS SEEM TO HAVE NOTICED...
GLANCE
!
JOLT

BADUMP BADUMP BADUMP
DID HE SEE?
FSHHH
NO...
I CAN'T BE SURE!
STARE
SENSEI FELL ASLEEP JUST NOW!
SAIKO
STAFF ROOM
EVERYTHING'S GETTING BLURRY...
I FEEL LIKE I COULD PASS OUT AT ANY MOMENT...
WOBBLE WOBBLE
Who ordered the tanuki?
Me!
OGATA UDON
Huff... Huff...
THANK GOODNESS WE HAVE REGULAR LESSONS IN THE AFTERNOON.
STANDING UP AND TALKING SHOULD BE BETTER...
OGATA UDON
HEY, KIRISU SENSEI ...
DID YOU HEAR ABOUT THIS AFTERNOON?
SLRRP
?

BABAM
THUS, I'D LIKE TO TAKE THIS OCCASION TO ADDRESS THE ENTIRE SCHOOL...
YAP YAP YAP
AS WE BEGIN THE SECOND SEMESTER, I AM PLEASED TO BLAH-DEE BLAH-DEE BLAH-BLAH...
YAP
YAP
YAP
SHEESH... A SCHOOL ASSEMBLY ALL AFTER-NOON...
YAP
THE PRINCIPAL SURE GOES ON FOR-EVER...
YAP
I GREW UP IN THE FOREST, YOU KNOW, AND...
YAP
...JUST THE OTHER DAY, A SWARM OF HERCULES BEETLES...
WHAT'S HE EVEN TALKING ABOUT?
IN OTHER WORDS, YOUNG PEOPLE THESE DAYS, ACCORDING TO STATIS-TICS...
YAP
YAP

WOBBLE
WOBBLE
THIS IS...
... HELL!!
M-MAFUYU ...
...HANG IN THERE!
YAP
YAP
YAP
A TEACHER'S JOB...
...IS TO SET AN EXAMPLE FOR THE STUDENTS!!
GRRRRIP
ZZZ
Ooog..
HANG ...
...IN ...
... THERE ...

AH-
CHOO!
AH-
CHOO!
JOLT
AHHH-
CHOO!!
PAH
BADUMP BADUMP BADUMP BADUMP BADUMP
TH-
THAT
STAR-
TLED
ME! YOU
OKAY,
NARI?
SNF
Y-YEAH.
JUST A
LITTLE
SNIFFLE
...
ZZZ
TEE
HEE
HEE
TH-
THAT
WAS
CLOSE
...
PHEW
...
SOMEHOW
I MADE IT
THROUGH
THE DAY...
BAM
Finally,
I can
sleep!
...

I WONDER ...
...IF YUIGA ...
SNF
...DID THAT TO SAVE ME?
NAH... I'M OVER-THINKING IT.
RUMMAGE
RUMMAGE
RUMMAGE
RUMMAGE
RUMMAGE
RUMMAGE
... NO WAY...
SHF...

UM, SENSEI ...
WHAT...
JOLT
IT'S NOTHING!
IT'S NOT NOTHING...
I LOST ...
...MY HOUSEKEY. MUST'VE DROPPED IT.
OH... OKAY...
I'M SURE I'LL FIND IT SOON. YOU GO ON HOME AND STUDY.
TOTTER TOTTER
SEN-SEI...
JOLT
W-WH...
Eep!
YOU AREN'T FEELING WELL TODAY, ARE YOU?
WHAT DO YOU MEAN?

POLICE
WORMP...
WELL, WE DIDN'T FIND IT.
NO...
I ALWAYS PUT IT IN MY JACKET POCKET.
WHERE COULD I HAVE DROPPED IT?

DID YOU REALLY DROP IT?
HOW ABOUT CHECKING YOUR BAG ONE MORE TIME?
OH, PLEASE.
RUMMAGE
I'VE CHECKED IT OVER AND OVER!
Mesopotamian Civilization
What is all this?
SPRAWL
MAN, WHATTA MESS!
DO YOU REALLY NEED ALL THIS STUFF?
WELL, EXCUSE ME!
THIS IS AN AMAZING DEVICE THAT MAKES SOFT-BOILED EGGS...
WHY NOT MAKE THEM AT HOME?
WHAT'S THIS?
Oh...
THAT'S NOTHING.
IT'S A USB MEMORY CASE.

Ha ha!
CHECK THIS OUT!
IT STORES SIX USB MEMORY STICKS! NICE, HUH?
CHK
Gee, you seem really proud of it...
KA
BAM

OH...
BAM
OH!!
SEVERAL HOURS EARLIER...
CHIRP
CHIRP
OOG... THE SUNLIGHT'S HARD TO TAKE...
RATTLE
RATTLE
SHAKA SHAKA
...BUT AT LEAST I'M ON TIME...
...
DID I REMEMBER THE USB...
...WITH THE MINI-TEST ON IT?
RUMMAGE
RUMMAGE
Can't forget that!
PERFECT!
PHEW
JUST IN CASE, I'LL CARRY IT BY HAND!
USB

END OF FLASHBACK..
...
STARE
SHAKA
SHAKA
SHAKA
BLUSH
...
...
SO...
...IT ALL GOES TO SHOW!
SHORT-TERM MEMORY DOESN'T LAST IF WE DON'T ASSOCIATE IT WITH SOMETHING!
ABSO-LUTELY!
THANKS FOR THAT LESSON, SENSEI!!
I REALLY...
...WANT TO THANK YOU FOR YOUR HELP TODAY...
... YUIGA.

NOT AT ALL.
I'M REALLY GLAD YOU FOUND YOUR KEY.
ANYWAY, I'LL BE GOING NOW...
WHUMP
...!
KSHH
ZZZ
SENSEI?!
WORLD HISTORY
Civilization Lesso
W-WHAT? SHE'S ASLEEP?!
AT LEAST GET INTO BED, SENSEI! YOU CAN DO IT!!
OH NO! SHE'S ALREADY DREAMING!!
Mumble... DON'T MAKE ME GO TO THE ASSEMBLY...
...OOG OO...
...
I'M SORRY, SENSEI...
FORGIVE ME.

...
SHE'S MORE DELICATE THAN I THOUGHT ...
...AND SO LIGHT ...
BADMP BADMP
ACK!
I'M SORRY!
I WASN'T THINKING ANYTHING WEIRD, I SWEAR!!
THE NEXT DAY...
CHIRP CHIRP
...
I DON'T REMEMBER ANYTHING AFTER GETTING HOME YESTER-DAY...
I CAN'T BELIEVE I MANAGED TO MAKE IT INTO BED ON MY OWN!
REFRESHED!
WELL DONE, ME!

What happened?
I fell asleep... and now my room's all clean?
Am I a genius?
GLEAM GLEAM
NAPOLEON AND THE HUNDRED DAYS

Question 57:
A Genius's New Look
Lands in [X]'s Blind Spot

I NEVER KNEW YOU CUT YOUR OWN HAIR, RICCHAN!
WHY NOT GO TO A SALON? YOU'RE A GIRL, AFTER ALL!
USUALLY I DON'T MESS UP.
IT MIGHT NOT SEEM LIKE IT, BUT I'M PRETTY GOOD AT IT.
MY LITTLE SISTER CUTS MY HAIR AT HOME TOO!
Wanna cut mine next time?
WHAT'S WRONG WITH THAT?
What?
SEE, FUMINO?
IT'S NORMAL!
TA-
DAAH!
SHKSHKSHKSHK
I'm my brother's barber...
Huh?
She's really skilled...
GULP
FUMI-NO!
YOU'RE RIGHT AFTER ALL!
I'LL GO TO A SALON NEXT TIME!

SALON'DE KARASUMA
SIGH...
· PRICE
PHEW ...
I CAN'T SEEM TO SHAKE THIS ENNUI, MAKIGAMI ...
OH DEAR, MISS KARASUMA. ARE YOU TIRED?
I SUPPOSE I'LL GO GET MY DELICATE CUTICLES TREATED SOMEWHERE...
Sigh...
IF ONLY WE COULD FIND A GIRL WHO'S LIKE AN UNCUT DIAMOND...
THAT OBSES- SION IS WHAT COSTS US OUR CUSTOMERS, BOSS!
Even though your skills are second to none...
SHOOSH
OH! WELCOME! COME IN!

EXCUSE ME...
THERE SHE IS! MY UNCUT DIAMOND!
WHAT ?!
SHE'S HERE! SHE'S HERE!
B-BOSS? CALM DOWN!
UM... MAY I COME IN?
OH, YES! EVERY-THING'S JUST FINE!
Listen up, Ricchan...
FUMINO CONVINCED ME...
...TO COME TO A SALON FOR THE FIRST TIME IN MY LIFE...

MY CREATIVE JUICES...
...ARE SWIRLING AND RISING LIKE A SPIRAL PERM!
OH, LOVELY! JUST PERFECT, MISS OGATA!!
ARE ALL SALONS LIKE THIS?
TWITCH
I RECOG-NIZE THAT SCENT ON THE TIPS OF YOUR LOCKS!
IT'S THE FRAGRANCE OF A YOUNG GIRL IN LOVE!!
WHY, DON'T TELL ME...
...YOU HAVE A DATE WITH A YOUNG MAN AFTER THIS?!
?
WELL, SORT OF...
A young girl in what?
I'M MEETING A FRIEND THIS AFTER-NOON TO STUDY IN THE LIBRARY...
WHAT ABOUT IT?
SIGH
UM... MISS KARA-SUMA... ARE YOU GONNA...?
YES, MURA-KAMI.
WE'RE PULLING OUT ALL THE STOPS.
??

A BODY PERM WITH EXTENSIONS, LASH EXTENSIONS, NATURAL MAKE-UP...
...AND OUR SIGNATURE EAU DE PARFUM!!
BAM
AND WE'LL CHOOSE THE PERFECT OUTFIT OUT OF MY OWN COLLECTION!
UM... THIS IS MY FIRST TIME AT A SALON, SO I DON'T REALLY KNOW...
IS THIS THE STANDARD PACKAGE?
I DON'T HAVE MUCH MONEY...
NEVER FEAR, DARLING!
WE'LL JUST CHARGE YOU THE BASIC CUT AND BLOW PRICE!
BOSS!!
CITY LIBRARY
OH...
OGATA SAID SHE'D BE HERE AROUND THIS TIME...
MAYBE HER APPOINTMENT THIS MORNING RAN LATE...

!
SHP
OH! THERE'S NARIYUKI!
SKRIT
SKRIT
Authors: Y~
GEE, THESE EXTENSION THINGIES MAKE MY HEAD HEAVY.
IT'S HARD TO WALK IN THESE HEELS...
AND I'VE NEVER LIKED WEARING CONTACTS...
THE ASSISTANT SEEMED ANGRY....
WONDER WHAT SHE MEANT ABOUT SALON POLICY...
SKRIT
SKRIT
WELL, ANYWAY...
TIME TO HIT THE BOOKS!
SHF
EXCUSE ME...
BOW
BOW

SPARKLE SPARKLE
KREAK
MM-HMM!
YEAH! I'M GOING TO GET GOOD MARKS TODAY...
...AND IMPRESS NARIYUKI!

WHO'S THIS?!
SHE'S SO CLOSE!
SHE'S SUPER BEAUTIFUL... AND SHE SMELLS AMAZING...
BA-DMP BA-DMP
BA-DMP BA-DMP
BUT NEVER MIND THAT!
THE LIBRARY'S FULL OF EMPTY SEATS! WHY HERE?!
DON'T TELL ME SHE'S...
BADMP BADMP
...HITTING ON ME?
THE STUFF OF URBAN LEGEND!
NO WAY. MAYBE IF I WERE GOOD-LOOKING LIKE KOBAYA-SHI...
MUST JUST BE SOME KINDA COINCI-DENCE.
GOTTA FOCUS ON STUDY-ING...
YOU OKAY?
SHP
YOUR FACE IS FLUSHED. ARE YOU RUNNING A FEVER?

SHE'S 100 PERCENT HITTING ON ME!!
36.4 DEGREES ...
NO FEVER
I'M EXPERIENCING AN URBAN LEGEND RIGHT NOW!!!
BA-DMP BA-DMP BA-DMP BA-DMP
PAH
EXCUSE ME!
THANK YOU FOR YOUR CONCERN, MISS, BUT I'M FEELING JUST FINE!!
Huh?
WHY SO FORMAL?
OGATA, WHERE ARE YOU?
I CAN'T HANDLE THIS!
BIP
!
PING
Nariyuki
YOU'RE SUPER LATE TODAY. EVERYTHING OKAY?
13:20

HE'S RIGHT!
I HAVEN'T SOLVED A SINGLE PROBLEM YET TODAY!
BUT... WHY IS HE TEXTING ME WHEN WE'RE RIGHT NEXT TO EACH OTHER?!
BA DMP
BA DMP
BA DMP
BA DMP
BA DMP
PLUS THE FORMAL LANGUAGE ...
SHVR
SEEMS LIKE HE'S BEING STRANGELY DISTANT...
OH!
LISTEN UP, OGATA!
WHEN A BOY SEES YOUR TRANSFORMATION AND GROWS SUDDENLY DISTANT, IT'S A SIGN!
IT'S A VERY GOOD SIGN, DEAR!
AN INDICATION THAT HE'S ENCHANTED BY YOUR TRANSFORMATION!

I THINK THAT MEANS WE'LL BECOME BETTER FRIENDS, RIGHT?
EN-CHANT-ED...
THAT'S QUITE ALL RIGHT. THIS IS A VERY GOOD SIGN, SO THERE'S ABSOLUTELY NO PROBLEM.
MM-HMM!
BIP
BIP
OH, OKAY. I'M CONFUSED, BUT...
SHE SAYS THERE'S NO PROBLEM, SO SHE MUST BE ON HER WAY...
ALL RIGHT!
WELL, NOW THAT I'VE MADE THAT BOLD DECLARATION...
I HAVE TO SOLVE THIS PROBLEM ON MY OWN!
SKRIT SKRIT SKRIT
OOOG...
I TOTALLY DON'T GET IT...
!
Question 5. Select the answer that best corresponds to the meaning of the following:
How didst thou attain such a beauteous countenance, m'lady?
(A) How did you get to be so beaut
(B) How did you get to be so manly
(C) How did you get to be so big?
(D) Nice muscles. How did you

THAT'S FROM "THE CHANGELINGS."
!
THE CHANGELINGS
"THE CHANGELINGS" IS THE STORY OF TWO CHILDREN, A GIRLISH BOY RAISED AS A PRINCESS AND A BOYISH GIRL RAISED AS A PRINCE.
Blush
OH. YES...
THIS PART ...
"HOW DIDST THOU ATTAIN SUCH A BEAUTEOUS COUNTE-NANCE, M'LADY?"
I REALLY DON'T GET IT.
THIS IS THE PART WHEN DAINAGON, THE FATHER, IS LAMENTING HOW BEAUTIFUL HIMEGIMI HAS GROWN, RIGHT?
THE CORRECT ANSWER IS A. "HOW DID YOU GET TO BE SO BEAUTIFUL?"
OH, I SEE...
BUT, WHAT'S WRONG WITH HIMEGIMI GROWING BEAU-TIFUL?
WELL, SEE...
HIME-GIMI WAS ORIGINALLY A BOY.
? ?
Huh?
Huh?
THEN WHY'S HE CALLED HIME-GIMI...?
...
THAT'S JUST THE PLOT OF THE STORY...

SHE REMINDS ME OF OGATA...!
WHAT IS IT?
O-OH! EXCUSE ME!
YOUR RESPONSE TO THE QUESTION REMINDED ME OF A GIRL I KNOW...
How rude of me!!
HEH
SHOOP
OH...
NEVER HEARD THAT BEFORE!
I CAN'T IMAGINE WHO HE MIGHT MEAN...
WHAT'S SHE LIKE?
WHAT ?!
WELL ...
You're super close!
LET'S SEE...
SHE'S ALWAYS TOTALLY GOING ALL OUT!
IF SHE DOESN'T UNDERSTAND SOMETHING, SHE HAS TO INVESTIGATE IT THROUGH AND THROUGH!
THE WAY SHE'S SO SERIOUS SHE'S SOMETIMES KINDA CLUELESS...
...AND THE WAY SHE'S STARTED SHOWING ALL SORTS OF FACIAL EXPRES-SIONS...

...IS JUST SO CUTE...
...THAT I CAN'T LEAVE HER ALONE.
SHE'S KINDA LIKE...
BADMP
...A SQUIRREL.
PHEW!
...?
BADMP BADMP
WHY WAS I RELIEVED JUST NOW?
FOR A MOMENT, MY CHEST FELT SO TIGHT...

COME TO THINK OF IT...
...
SKRIT SKRIT
SOMETHING DOESN'T FEEL QUITE RIGHT.
WHY DO I FEEL SO UNSETTLED AND IRRITATED?
GASP
...!
COME TO THINK OF IT...
A LOT OF GUYS ARE SHY...
...SO YOU'VE GOT TO BE SURE TO ASK HIM THIS QUES-TION...
UM...
HOW DO I...
...STRIKE YOU...
...TODAY?
UM ...
FINE!
ONCE YOU GET THE PATTERNS DOWN, ANCIENT TEXTS AREN'T TOO HARD...

SKOOT
AIEEE!!
HOW! DO I!
TODAY?! STRIKE YOU!
WHY ARE YOU LOOKING AWAY?!
WELL, UH, I MEAN...
I DON'T KNOW WHAT YOU MEAN!!
SHE'S TOO GORGEOUS... I CAN'T LOOK HER IN THE EYES UP CLOSE!
WHY'S SHE BEING SO AGGRESSIVE WHEN WE'VE NEVER EVEN MET BEFORE?!
BLUSH
GETTING HIT ON BY A GIRL...
...IS WAY SCARIER THAN I THOUGHT!
SHH! QUIET VOICES IN THE LIBRARY, PLEASE!
S-SORRY!

CITY LIBRARY
THE LIBRARY IS NOW CLOSING...
SHEESH.. I'M BEAT...
TMP
OGATA NEVER SHOWED. WONDER WHAT HAPPENED...
SHAH
AND HOW LONG...
...IS THIS PERSON GONNA STICK AROUND?
...
WEIRD...
MAYBE IT'S JUST ME...
...BUT IT DOESN'T FEEL LIKE OUR FRIEND-SHIP HAS DEEPENED...
I GUESS IT'S TIME...
I'LL GIVE YOU THE FINAL TRUMP CARD!
WORKS EVERY TIME— THERE ISN'T A BOY ON EARTH WHO ISN'T SUSCEP-TIBLE!
TADA
ER...

WOULD YOU CARE TO STOP BY MY PLACE?
BLRFOO
KOFF
CHOKE GACK
LISTEN, YOU SHOULD HAVE MORE RESPECT FOR YOUR-SELF!
IF YOU GO AROUND INVITING GUYS OVER SO LIGHTLY, IMAGINE HOW YOUR PARENTS WILL FEEL!
?
HONESTLY, I THINK THEY WORRY THAT I NEVER HAVE ANY-ONE OVER.
WHAA-AT?!
ALL RIGHT.
WHERE'S YOUR HOUSE?
I THINK IT'S BEST...
...IF I HAVE A LITTLE CHAT WITH YOUR PARENTS!

OGATA UDON
R R R M M B B B
YES, SEN-SEI?
YOU WANTED TO HAVE A TALK WITH ME?
R R M
HERE'S YOUR OGATA UDON!
ENJOY!
B B B
IT'S NOTH-ING...

WELL... I SEE YOUR DAUGHTER HAS UNDERGONE A MAKEOVER...
QUIVER QUIVER
SHE SURE HAS!
SHAKA SHAKA
DON'T YOU DARE FALL IN LOVE, NOW!
GLANCE
?
BLUSH
WHAT'S WRONG?
OGATA UDON
"HOW ...
...DIDST THOU ATTAIN SUCH A BEAUTEOUS COUNTE-NANCE?"
TREMBL TREMBL
OH!
YOU'RE QUOTING "THE CHANGELINGS," NARIYUKI!
"NARI-YUKI"?!

I detect the aroma of dangerous love!
A rough, uncut diamond!
Chill out, boss.

VWHOO
Question 58:
On a Stormy Night, a Genius's Heart Isn't in [X]
TYPHOON 18 CONTINUES TO GAIN INTENSITY...
...AND WILL STRIKE THE TOKYO AREA AT 5 P.M. TODAY...
ESPRIT
NEWS
THEY CANCELED OUR AFTERNOON CLASSES!
NICE! ♪
RTL RTL
WELL, SINCE WE HAVE THE AFTERNOON OFF...
...I'LL HAVE LOTS OF TIME TO PREPARE LESSONS FOR THE GIRLS...
!
VWHOO
RTL RTL

...
WHAT'S UP, FURUHASHI? YOU SEEM PREOCCUPIED.
WE SHOULD HEAD HOME BEFORE THE STORM STARTS.
OH! YUIGA!
Y-YEAH, YOU'RE RIGHT!
WE REALLY SHOULD GET GOING!
VWHOOO
?
GAH!
MY HAIR'S A MESS... AND MY SKIRT...
VWHOOO
THE RAIN COULD STARTANY MINUTE...
OH!

jomosan
I NEED TO MAKE A QUICK STOP. BYE!
VWHOOO
SEE YOU, YUIGA!
DID YOU HEAR WHAT I JUST SAID?!
DO YOU EVEN HAVE AN UMBRELLA?!
YOU SHOULD GO STRAIGHT HOME!
VWHOOO
NO... HA HA HA!
I GUESS I JUST DON'T REALLY FEEL LIKE GOING HOME YET...
GEE...
YOU REALLY DON'T NEED TO KEEP ME COMPANY, YUIGA...
WELL, I'M ACTUALLY HUNGRY TOO...
What's cheap here?
HEY, I FEEL KINDA WORKED UP, WHAT WITH THE TYPHOON AND ALL...
LET'S BOTH GET THE DELUXE PARFAIT—MY TREAT!
DELUXE PARFAIT
3,500
IT'S 3,500 YEN?!
Ha ha ha!
I'VE GOT IT COVERED!
EXCUSE ME!
Thanks, Fumino!

SHAKA
EXCUSE ME...
TREMBL TREMBL
I'M AFRAID WE'RE CLOSING NOW DUE TO THE TYPHOON...
SHAKA SHAKA
STEAKHOUSE PEKKOPEKO
BAM
CLOSED
SUSHI
BAM
Closed for the Day
EEL
BAM
CLOSED
BAM
NISSOM
UMAI
SLRR RRRP

PappyMar
VWHOOOO
SLRRP
SLRRP
SLRRP
SLRRP
NOW HIRING
ATM
WAAAH
JOLT
THIS ISN'T CUTTING IT!
THIS AIN'T CUTTIN' IT!
I WAS FIXIN' TO SPLURGE AND REALLY CUT LOOSE TODAY!
CALM DOWN! WHAT'S WITH THE WEIRD ACCENT ?!
WHAT, YOU DON'T LIKE INSTANT NOO-DLES?!
DRIP DRIP
UMAI RAMEN
Gah!
RAGE RAGE
I LOVE THEM! DUH!
CAN I TASTE YOUR SEA-FOOD-FLAVORED ONE?
LET'S SWAP!
...
What's up?!
UMAI RAMEN
Seafood
GASP

WAIT A SEC...
SLRRP
This is yummy too! ♥
BADMP
SHE ATE WITH THESE CHOPSTICKS ALREADY!
SO THIS IS...
...AN INDIRECT KISS...
VWH
OOO
OH!
AAAH!
VWHOO
SPLK
OH! SORRY!
PATTER PATTER
HUH?
YEEK! THE RAIN'S STARTING!
QUICK! EAT FASTER, YUIGA!
THE RAIN WILL MAKE THE SOUP COLD!
SHAAAAA
IS THAT SERIOUSLY THE PRIMARY ISSUE RIGHT NOW?!

SHO OSH
SPLASHA
SPLASHA
THIS IS INTENSE!
BATTER BATTER
BATTER BATTER
I-I'M SORRY... IT'S MY FAULT...
YOU WANTED TO GO HOME EARLIER...
I REALLY DON'T MIND.
I'M JUST CONCERNED ...
YOU SEEM LIKE SOME-THING'S UP WITH YOU TODAY.
...
NOT REALLY ...

MY DAD'S AT HOME TODAY...
SO I KINDA...
...DON'T WANNA GO HOME.
SKRTCH
MAYBE ...
...WE COULD ...
...LOOK FOR SOME-WHERE TO GET OUT OF THE RAIN...

THAT'S OKAY.
I DON'T WANT TO CAUSE YOU ANY MORE TROUBLE.
I CAN JUST GO HOME.
BUT ... THANK YOU.
YOU'RE REALLY KIND...
...NARI-YUKI.
IT'S NO PROB-LEM.
OH...
HUH?
OH...
COME TO THINK OF IT, THIS SITUATION ...
TWO LOVERS UNDER AN UM-BRELLA ...
VWHOOO

VWSHHH
?!
SHAAAA
LET'S...
YES.
LET'S FIND SHELTER...
KSHHH
RETRO CINEMA
PHILIACINEMA
PHEW!

GEEZ, THAT WAS BRUTAL...
TOTALLY EMPTY...
AH HA HA... WELL, WE'VE GOT THIS PLACE ALL TO OURSELVES!
THERE'S POPCORN, EVEN!
YAY!
HMM ...
RATTLE RATTLE
KREAK KREAK
I HOPE THIS MOVIE THEATER IS SOLID...
BADMP BADMP
HEY, LOOK, YUIGA!
THEY'RE SHOWING A REALLY OLD MOVIE!
I've never seen it!
YAY!
OH...BUT IT LOOKS A LITTLE SCARY.
ARE YOU OKAY WITH THAT?
YEAH, SURE ...
IF IT'S NOT SUPER SCARY.

AA
AA
A
KRUNCH KRUNCH
AA
OH NOOO!!
HELP!!!
KRUNCH KRUNCH
AAAAAAH!
THIS IS...
...SUPER SCARY!!
A "LITTLE" SCARY?
OGATA WOULD'VE DIED SEVEN TIMES BY NOW!
GLANCE
...
Hmm. That zombie person wasn't wearing make-up.
MUNCH MUNCH
GEE, FURU-HASHI SURE IS TOUGH!

SHRAK
KRAKLE KRAKLE KRAKLE
POP
HUH ?!
WHAT ?!
W-W-WHAT NOW ?!
DID THEY GET BEHIND ON THE ELECTRICITY BILL?
IS THIS PART OF THE MOVIE?
SEEMS KINDA LONG...
KCHAK
I'M T-TERRIBLY SORRY!
THE POWER WENT OUT WITH THAT LAST THUNDER-CLAP...
!
WE'LL RESTORE THE FILM AS SOON AS WE CAN... WOULD YOU MIND WAITING?
OH... SURE!
THE LIGHTNING TOOK OUT THE POWER!
WOW ...
I GUESS THAT ACTU-ALLY HAP-PENS!

TOUCH...
JOLT
HUH?
OH!
SORRY... I COULDN'T SEE...
I GUESS... I'M A LITTLE SCARED.
COULD WE TALK A BIT?
OKAY. WHAT'S THE FORMULA FOR THE ADDITION THEOREM OF A TANGENT?
GLEAM
$\tan(\alpha \pm \beta) = \frac{\tan\alpha \pm \tan\beta}{1 \mp \tan\alpha\tan\beta}$
THAT'S NOT EXACTLY WHAT I MEANT BY TALK...
BUT WOW! YOU REALLY KNEW IT!
Heh heh
WELL, YEAH!
GO AHEAD, ASK ME ANY-THING!
Maybe...

OKAY. NEXT...
...
TELL ME...
...ABOUT...
...YOUR FATHER.
YOU DON'T HAVE TO...
...OF COURSE.
I CAN'T.
EVEN IF I TOLD YOU...
...YOU'D NEVER BELIEVE ME.
...
I SEE.
OKAY.
...
WELL, ANYWAY...

THIS SURE HAS BEEN ...
...A WEIRD DAY!
HA HA!
THAT'S FOR SURE!
WE WENT AROUND TO ALL THOSE RESTAURANTS...
THE CUP RAMEN INCIDENT ...
GETTING CAUGHT IN THE RAIN....
OUR UMBRELLA BREAKING, GETTING SOAKED!
FINALLY FINDING A MOVIE THEATER ...
...AND THE POWER GOING OUT!
IT'S ALL MY FAULT. I'M SORRY.
GOSH, WHAT A DAY...
OH!

IT'S LIKE A DATE!
ISN'T IT, FURUHASHI?!

YES.
YAY! ♪
SPLISH
HEY, NOW! YOU'LL GET WET AGAIN!
ARE YOU... OKAY GOING HOME NOW?
YEAH! A LITTLE MORE WATER HARDLY MAKES A DIFFERENCE NOW!
SPLISH
SPLISH
BESIDES, BY NOW MY DAD WILL BE ASLEEP.
LET'S HEAD HOME, NARIYUKI!
?
I DON'T REALLY GET IT, BUT...
...SHE SEEMS HAPPIER NOW...
...SO THAT'S GOOD!
?

THE NEXT DAY...
3-A
HEY, FURU-HASHI!
WHAT?
IF YOU WERE GONNA GO ON A DATE...
...WOULDN'T YOU WANT TO GO TO A FRENCH RESTAU-RANT? ♡
NO WAY! I'D GO FOR JAPANESE FOOD! A TRADITIONAL-STYLE PLACE!
DON'TCHA THINK, FURU-HASHI?
Weekends for Lovers
French Themed Special
Food Mania
Lovely Japanese Sweets!
FRENCH!
JAPANESE!
...
HOW ABOUT INSTANT NOODLES AT A CONVE-NIENCE SHOP?
WHAAAT? IS THAT A JOKE?

DON'T BE RIDICULOUS! WE CAN'T DO DELIVERIES TODAY!
HEY!
GOING OUT ON DELIVERIES NOW!
SHFF
VWHOOO
RIZURIN, COME BACK!!

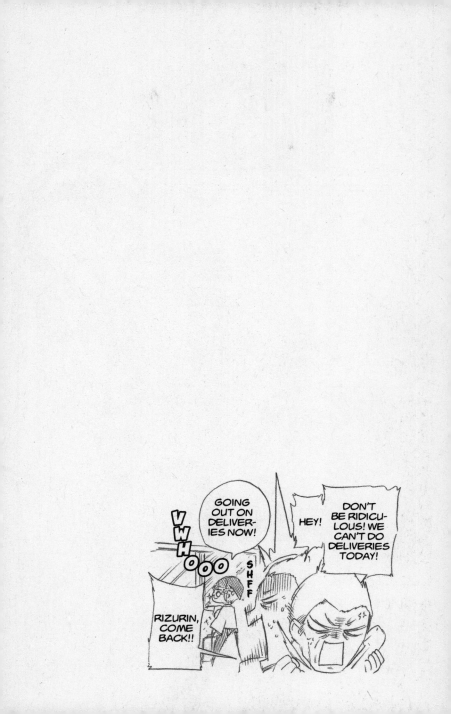

Question 59: Sometimes a Genius Struggles with a Limited [X]

WERE YOU OKAY THE OTHER DAY, WITH THE TYPHOON?
THE CARRYING CASE GOT BLOWN AWAY, SO IT WAS HARD TO MAKE DELIVERIES.
YOU WERE MAKING DELIV-ERIES?!
Sounds dangerous!
!
Burnable Garbage
Burnable Garbage
U-URUKA AND NARI-YUKI...
BDM
LOOKS LIKE A SERIOUS, PRIVATE CONVER-SATION...
DON'T TELL ME THEY'RE MAKING A...
This ...

This is a notebook!
BLUSH
R
Yes!
It's your home-work notebook!
CAN IT BE...?
?
I-it's so white!
So beautiful!
BLAH BLAH
...
WHAT'S GOING ON?
SEVERAL HOURS EARLIER ...
LIBRARY
OH...
Name

WOW, YOU'VE LEARNED A LOT OF ENGLISH VOCAB!
YOU'VE REALLY BEEN WORKING HARD!
YAY! VALI-DATION!
HA HA HA!
I THINK IT'S TIME ...
...TO PRACTICE SPEAKING MORE.
I need practice too.
TRUE. THERE'S AN ENGLISH INTERVIEW IN THE ENTRANCE EXAM FOR OTOWA UNIVERSITY.
HEH HEH, NARIYUKI!
YOU MIGHT NOT BELIEVE THIS...
...BUT I PRACTICE SPEAKING EVERY DAY WITH MY MOM!
I'VE GOT IT COVERED!
Why are you interested in our col-lege?
WOW! THAT'S GREAT, URUKA!
AHEM!
WELL THEN ...
Please introduce yourself.

My...
M-my n-name is...
UH
ER
STAMMER
Take-moto Uruka!
I MEAN ...
NOT THAT!
Uruka Take-moto!
I swim ...
SWIM SWIM
... very... very...
UM...
BAM
Mega-High!
SQUEEZE
AND— UM...
I LIKE ...
CHOP CHOP CHOP ...
SIZZ... SIZZ...
SIZ-ZLE...
TON TON
OH! RIGHT!
Cook-ing!
SO GOOD!
YUM YUM!
CHATTER CHATTER
Bravo! ♡
Th-thank you!

KASLAM
WAH! NARI-YUKI?!
YOU'RE SO NERVOUS!
WHAT HAPPENED TO YOUR CONFI-DENCE?!
I-I CAN'T HELP IT!
I FEEL REALLY SHY SPEAKING ENGLISH! VERY, VERY NERVOUS!
WHAT'S WITH THE JAPAN-GLISH ?!
ANYWAY ...
I THINK YOUR MAIN ISSUE ISN'T GRAMMAR.
...
SLUMP
English is scary.
English is scary.
English is scary.
IT'S THAT YOU GET ALL PANICKED AND ROBOTIC...
WHAP
OKAY!
...

IN ORDER TO BOOST YOUR CONFI-DENCE...
...HOW ABOUT IF WE ONLY SPEAK ENGLISH TODAY?
WHAT?!
YOU'VE GOTTA BE KID-DING!
ALL DAY?!
THAT'S SO EMBAR-RASSING!
DOES THAT MEAN...
...WE'RE GOING TO BE TOGETHER ALL DAY?!
Good night, Uruka.
*OF COURSE NOT.
WHOEVER RESORTS TO JAPANESE FIRST HAS TO BUY THE OTHER ONE A STEAMED BUN!
SURE, COUNT ME IN!
OH, IS THAT SO? YOU SEEM PRETTY CONFI-DENT!

WHICH BRINGS US TO NOW...
FWHSH
CHIRP CHIRP
It's such a fine day. Don't you think so?
Uh... I'm fine!
SHE STILL SEEMS AWFULLY NERVOUS.
I WISH SHE COULD RELAX A BIT.
AWKWARDNESS
She's swing-ing her left arm when she steps with her left foot!
STIFF STIFF
SWISH
!

YAP!
RUB RUB
OH!
Do-do-do...
Dog!
It's a dog! Nariyuki!!
PAT PAT
Very, very, very cuuuuute!

Do you like dogs?
Yes!
So lovely!
LICK LICK
UMM...
Where are you from?
What is your name?
AWW!
LICK LICK
Uruka!
Your language skills are excellent.

Your lingerie is excellent.
HEH...
TMP
WHAA-AAAT?!
You are perverted!
BLUSH
Why?!
PANIC PANIC
NO WAY! DID HE SEE MY UNDIES?
DID I WEAR CUTE ONES TODAY?
WAIT... THAT'S NOT THE POINT!
?

What do you mean?! I'm not perverted!
Very, very perverted!
I am not!
GYAA GYAA
BLUSH
Mama, it's them again!
WHAT AN EMBARRASSING CONVERSATION...
SCOWL
Prove it!
BLUSH
Prove?!
WHAT?!
GEEZ... SHE'S USING SOME REALLY GOOD VOCAB!
Of course!
I'm not perverted because...
BLOOP BLOOP BLOOP BLOOP
...
I...
I give up!
!

GLOW
WAIT A MINUTE ...
YOU GIVE UP?
YAY! I WIIIIN!
OH! URUKA!
YOU LOSE! YOU SPOKE JAPANESE FIRST!
I said "I give up" in English!
WHAA-AAAAT?! NO WAY !!
*"GIVE UP" IS USED IN JAPANESE, TOO!
NO FAIR! YOU TRICKED ME!
SORRY, URUKA. RULES ARE RULES!
WHEW! AT LEAST WE'RE OFF THAT TOPIC!
100
OKAY. I'LL GO GET THE BUNS!
I'm having a curry bun!
I WANT A PIZZA BUN!
GOT IT!

Arf arf arf!
Good doggy!
Excuse me.
Could you tell me the way to Ichinose Station?
BABAM
YIIIIIKES!
BLAH-DEE-BLAH-DEE-BLAH
FREEZE
UM, THEY'RE ASKING THE WAY TO THE STATION, RIGHT?
I think...
G-go straight!
And right! Right!
At...the po...the post office!
DRIP DRIP
GESTURE GESTURE

Okay!
Thank you very much!
THEY UNDER-STAND!
RIGHT ON!
BLOOSH
Well then... we'll have a barbecue party with friends.
BLAH DEE BLAH DEE
Would you like to join us, you beautiful, nice lady?
WHA...
BLAH-DEE
BLAH-DEE
BLAH-BLAH
WHA ...
WHAT ?!
BLAH-DEE-BLAH-DEE-BLAH
WOW, I COMMUNICATED WITH FOREIGNERS!
MAYBE I'M ACTUALLY PRETTY TALENTED ...
BLAH-DEE-BLAH...
HUH ?
BLAH-BLAH
BLAH-DEE BLAH-DEE
Y-YIKES!!
ARE THEY TRYING TO PICK ME UP?!
N-n-no...th-thank... you!
BLAH DEE BLAH DEE
I…w-wait... for… friend ...
DRIP DRIP
SHOOP

HEY!
WHAT DO YOU THINK YOU'RE DOING?!
SHOOP
NARI-YUKI!
BA-DMP
What's the relationship between you two?
Hmm?
JOLT
WE, UM... ER...
NO... NO NEED TO BE AFRAID OF FOR-EIGN-ERS!
WHY NOT JUST TELL THE TRUTH?
She is my precious study friend...
THAT'S IT!!
SHE...
She is...

She is my...
...precious steady!!
[STEADY]
1. STABLE, UNCHANGING
2. A PARTNER ONE DATES EXCLUSIVELY (AS IN "TO GO STEADY")
DID I SAY THAT WRONG?
TAKA TAKA TAKA

HA HAHAHA
Oh! I'm sorry!
She's a gorgeous girl... Shoulda known she'd be taken!
Take good care of her, buddy!
Good luck!
FWEET-FWOO ♪
OH!
OKAY... BYE...
THAT LAST PART...
...WAS TOO FAST. I COULDN'T CATCH IT.
What was that about?
WELL ANYWAY, I'M GLAD YOU'RE OKAY.
ARE YOU OKAY, URUKA?
...
art

NOD NOD
GULP
GULP
AAH
AAH
AAH
...
AAH
SMILE SMILE
STRETCH
STRETCH
SWF
SWF
SHOOP
SHOOP
SHOOP
STRETCH
STREEETCH
STREEETCH
TAP TAP

ZOOOSH
What?!
WHERE ARE YOU GOING?!
AND WHY'D YOU SUDDENLY LOSE THE ABILITY TO SPEAK?!
DON'T LOOK AT ME NOW!
COME BACK, URUKA!
LATER...
My homework notebook is very white!
Every day!
Oh, yay!
...
HMM. WELL, YOU SEEM TO HAVE LOST YOUR SHY-NESS ABOUT SPEAKING ENGLISH...
Oh, yay?
CONTENT STILL NEEDS WORK, THOUGH.
Is that what you'll say in your interview?

Did you play with a nice human, woof?
Yes, Mama, woof!
That human was so bad at English I almost corrected fur!
Haah
Haah
Now, you know we can't do that! We have to pretend we don't under-stand!
*SEE VOLUME 6.

Question 60: Sometimes a Predecessor's [X] Becomes His Sacrifice
CHIRP
CHIRP
Nanao Library
WELL, IF IT ISN'T THE RUNT!
KOMI-NAMI SENPAI!
PERFECT TIMING!

OOG ...
SORRY, KIDDO...
SHALL I GIVE YOU A HUG FOR REACHING IT FOR ME?
WHAT ...?!
GAH
YOU DON'T HAVE TO DO THAT!!
HEH
A...
ALMOST GOT IT...
SHP
928
テ
G...
GOT...
SHF
?!
OH!

SHOOOP
KIDDO!
WATCH OUT!
KOMINAMI CLINIC
IT'S A MINOR SPRAIN.
SHOULD BE ALL BETTER IN THREE WEEKS.

ANY-WAY...
BE SURE TO TAKE IT EASY FOR A FEW DAYS.
YIKES!!
I'M SO SORRY, SENPAI! IT'S ALL MY FAULT!
IT'S NOT MY DOMINANT HAND, SO I'LL BE FINE.
I'M THE ONE WHO MESSED UP. DON'T WORRY ABOUT IT.
TH...
THAT'S NOT POSSIBLE!
THIS IS MY FAULT. I'M GOING TO STICK TO YOU LIKE GLUE AND TAKE CARE OF YOU!
DON'T TREAT ME LIKE AN INVALID!
...
BADMP
OH, SON... ♡
ASUMI
SKRIT
...
SKRIT
SKRIT

LOOM
TMP
HEY, KID...
DON'T WORRY! I'LL HOLD YOUR NOTEBOOK STEADY FOR YOU!
BAM
OH! NEED HELP ERASING SOME-THING?
OR REPLACING THE GRAPHITE IN YOUR MECHANICAL PENCIL?
WHAT-EVER YOU NEED, JUST SAY IT!
OH MY GOD, YOU'RE BEING SO OVER-BEAR-ING!
I TOLD YOU, JUST FORGET ABOUT THIS!
DO YOUR OWN STUDY-ING!
EEP!
BUT HE SAID IT'LL TAKE THREE WEEKS TO HEAL!
MY DAD'S ALWAYS EXAGGER-ATING!
IT HARDLY EVEN HURTS!
HEH
YOU'RE REALLY DOWN TO HELP ME WITH WHATEVER I WANT?
SHP
O-OF COURSE!

HERE! OPEN UP!
GO ON! YOU'RE MY BOYFRIEND—FEED ME LIKE YOU ALWAYS DO!
YOU KNOW, LIKE USUAL!
TREMBL TREMBL
BLUSH
SIRRP SIRRP
TREMBL TREMBL
ER, EXCUSE ME...
YOUR RIGHT HAND'S NOT INJURED... SO CAN'T YOU FEED YOURSELF?
PSST PSST
BADMP BADMP
YOU SAID YOU'D DO ANY-THING.
THIS IS ALSO AN ACT FOR MY DAD, SO TRY TO GET INTO CHARAC-TER!
PHYSICS
YES, BUT...
THIS IS SO EMBAR-RASSING...
For real...

AUGH!
CHOMP
SLRP
SLRP
SLLRP
OMG!
SLRRRP
TP TP
More! More!
WHAT'S SHE DOING?
Yum, yum!
THERE'S NO WAY HER DAD LIKES THIS...
...
SLRRRP
BADMP BADMP
...
SLRRRP
WHAT TO DO ...
A CHURCH WEDDING? OR A SHINTO SHRINE?
BAM
SO HARD TO DECIDE!!

ALL RIGHT.
Thank you.
Thank you.
SHALL WE BE GOING SOON?
BLUSH
HUH?
BA BAM
BAM
WELCOME BACK, DARLING! ♡
JUST WHAT DO YOU THINK YOU'RE DOING?!
GUH!

I CAN'T JUST DITCH MY SHIFT!
You're making a scene!
But...
Your left hand...
I'M TELLING YOU, IT BARELY HURTS!
IN FACT, WORK IS EASIER NOW BECAUSE EVERYONE FUSSES OVER ME!
Oh! What happened to your hand, Ashumi?
Oh, just a little injury!
Please pardon me for only using my right hand today!
MAYBE I'M WORRYING TOO MUCH...
SHE SEEMS TO BE DOING PRETTY WELL, ACTUALLY...
That'll be 240 yen.
SAIKO
OKAY...
TIME FOR MY 30 MINUTE BREAK-SY! ♡
HM?
ASHUMI ALREADY WENT BACK TO THE BREAK ROOM?
HERE, YUIGA, WILL YOU TAKE HER THIS MEAL?
Sure!
TMP TMP

ER...
SEN ...
OUCH!
PATTER
?!
OOOG ...
GEEZ, THAT HURTS. ARG...
KRNK

UM...
LET'S SEE... THE FORMULA FOR THE PERIOD OF AN OBJECT MOVING IN A UNIFORM CIRCULAR MOTION...
$T = \frac{2\pi}{\omega}$
THE NUMBER OF REVOLUTIONS IS...
$n = \frac{1}{T} = \frac{\omega}{2\pi}$
FWIP
DARN... IT'S HARD TO TURN THESE!
ITS ROTATIONAL VELOCITY IS...
SWF
OUCH!
I'M TELLING YOU, IT BARELY HURTS!
IN FACT, WORK IS EASIER NOW BECAUSE EVERYONE FUSSES OVER ME!
$v = r\omega$
OW-OW-OW...
$U = \frac{3}{2} nRT$
$a = r\omega^2 = \frac{v^2}{r}$
OH, DRAT...
I FORGET THIS ONE...

KOMINAMI CLINIC
TMP TMP TMP
TMP TMP TMP TMP
SENPAI! I FINISHED CLEANING THE ENTIRE HOUSE!
OH! THANKS.
HERE! I BROUGHT YOU SOME TEA!
SUG-AR?
MILK?
HOW ABOUT A SLICE OF LEMON?
UM, KIDDO?
IT FEELS LIKE YOU'RE MORE OVER-BEARING THAN EVER NOW... DID SOMETHING HAPPEN?
NOT AT ALL!
SHALL I TURN THE PAGES OF YOUR BOOK?
THAT'S WHAT I MEAN BY OVER-BEARING!

Okay; I'll just organize these books...
...
GEE...
I GOT ALL SWEATY AT WORK TONIGHT!
BUT I'M NOT SUPPOSED TO BATHE FOR AT LEAST ANOTHER DAY...
I KNOW, KOHAI...
YOU CAN SPONGE DOWN MY BACK FOR ME.
OF COURSE ...
YOU'LL HAVE TO UNDO MY BRA FIRST.

IF YOU CAN'T HELP ME WITH THAT, YOU SHOULD GO NOW.
BAM
FINE!
PCHAK
FLP
SLOSH SLOSH
SKWEEZ
HUH? ARE YOU SERIOUS?!
Also, you seem pretty slick at undoing a bra!
OH!
RIGHT... PLEASE EXCUSE ME! I WASN'T THINKING!
DON'T WORRY! I'LL WEAR A BLIND-FOLD!
SHOOP
UM, THAT'S NOT THE ISSUE...
WHO ARE YOU?! ARE YOU REALLY THE RUNT I KNOW?!

OOH ...
COLD ...
...
GEE...
YOU'RE SURPRIS-INGLY BOLD SOME-TIMES.
FURU-HASHI IS ALWAYS LECTUR-ING ME...
...ABOUT NOT UNDER-STANDING FEMININE PSYCHOLOGY.
OH?
What's this about?
YOU KNOW...
I DO NEED YOU TO TELL ME STUFF. OTHERWISE I DON'T KNOW.

WHEN YOU'RE IN PAIN AND YOU PRETEND YOU'RE NOT...
...I FEEL BAD.
EVEN THOUGH IT'S JUST PRE-TEND...
AS YOUR BOYFRIEND, I MEAN.
SHEESH...
SOME-TIMES YOU REALLY SAY STUFF...
...THAT THROWS ME.
HUH?
NOTHING!
IF YOU'RE GONNA SPONGE ME DOWN, DO IT PROPERLY!

SORRY! YOU MEAN LIKE THIS?
OUCH!
OUCH! THAT'S TOO STRONG, YOU DUMMY!
I'M A GIRL! BE A LITTLE MORE DELICATE, WOULDJA?!
THUMP
BOMP
THUMP
SLRRP
TNK
I WONDER...
...IF I'LL BE A GRANDFATHER SOON!
Heh heh heh heh
I'D SURE LIKE FOUR...
...GRANDCHILDREN!
THE NEXT DAY...
Nanao Library

HEY THERE! HITTING THE BOOKS, HUH?
OH!
HI, KOMINAMI SENPAI!
JOLT
?
IS SOME-THING WRONG, NARIYUKI?
TREMBL TREMBL
OH...
I'M FINE...
Is your hand okay?
Yep.
GOTTA CALM DOWN... CALM DOWN...
TREMBL TREMBL TREMBL
I GOT TOTALLY CARRIED AWAY THAT DAY...
...AND DID SOME REALLY EMBAR-RASSING STUFF!
Heh...
?
JOLT
WHY SO FLUSTERED, KIDDO?

PAT
I REALLY DIDN'T MIND IT...
HOW BOLD YOU WERE THAT NIGHT...
HEH HEH HEH
MY... ♪
... SPONGE BATH MAN!♡
POOF
DON'T CALL ME THAT! IT SOUNDS LIKE SPONGE-BOB!
YEAH, THAT'S THE SPIRIT!
I DO LOVE GETTING A RISE OUT OF YOU, KOHAI!
?
SPONGE BATH...?

GRANDCHILD
NAMING
DICTIONARY

We Never Learn 7

STAFF LIST

STAFF

Taishi Tsutsui

Yu Kato

Naoki Ochiai

Sachiko

Yukki

Satoshi Okazaki

HELP

Paripoi

Kazuya Higuchi

Fuka Toma

Chikomichi

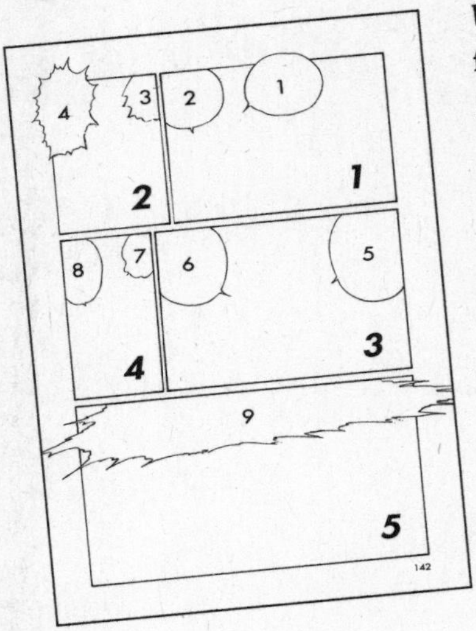

We Never Learn reads from right to left, starting in the upper-right corner. Japanese is read from right to left, meaning that action, sound effects and word-balloon order are completely reversed from English order.